MYTHS

A · N · D

REALITIES

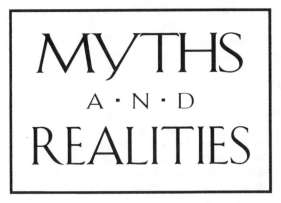

MYTHS A·N·D REALITIES

BEST PRACTICES FOR LANGUAGE MINORITY STUDENTS

KATHARINE DAVIES SAMWAY
A • N • D
DENISE MCKEON

HEINEMANN
PORTSMOUTH, NH

Heinemann
A division of Reed Elsevier Inc.
361 Hanover Street
Portsmouth, NH 03801–3912
http://www.heinemann.com

Offices and agents throughout the world

Library of Congress Cataloging-in-Publication Data
Samway, Katharine Davies.
    Myths and realities: best practices for language minority students / Katharine Davies Samway and Denise McKeon.
        p.   cm.
    Includes bibliographical references (p. 113) and index.
    ISBN 0-325-00057-3
        1. Linguistic minorities—Education—United States.   2. Linguistic minorities—Services for—United States.   3. Education, Bilingual—United States.
    I.   McKeon, Denise.   II.   Title.
    LC3731.S25   1999
    370.117'5'0973—dc21   98-50063
                                                                                                          CIP

Editor: Lois Bridges
Production: Elizabeth Valway
Cover design: Jenny Jensen Greenleaf
Manufacturing: Louise Richardson

Printed in the United States of America on acid-free paper

07 06 05 04   DA   10 11 12 13 14

Contents

Acknowledgments

We feel very grateful to have had support from so many people while writing this book. In particular, we extend our heartfelt thanks to

- Barbara Agor, Tim Beard, Jill Dempster, Dan Doorn, Marty Krovetz, Cindy Moore, Melinda Nettles, Heather Sellens, Dorothy Taylor, and María Wetzel, whose comments and suggestions helped us to define the content of the book.
- Cindy Pease-Alvarez, who read an early draft of the book and provided us with thoughtful, invaluable feedback.
- Tom Samway, who read an almost complete draft; his detailed comments and questions helped us answer some of the issues that we had not yet resolved.
- Lois Bridges, who has been a supportive and resourceful editor throughout the writing of the book.

Also a special thanks to Holly . . . the dog who *didn't* eat the homework.

Introduction

This is a book that provides good, solid research information about programs and practices that have proven to be effective for helping language minority students achieve academically. As we set about writing, however, we realized that many mainstream educators (those who have not been specially trained to work with language minority and limited English-proficient students) might first need some basic background information about language acquisition, legal requirements for educating linguistically diverse students, and placement, program, and assessment information that would guide them through a new and emerging climate of high-stakes accountability.

Both of us have spent a considerable portion of our professional careers providing inservice training, technical assistance, and professional development to mainstream educators, trying to help them cope with shifting demographics, new demands for professional preparation, and the changing realities of public schools in the United States. We realized that in our interactions with educators, we had often heard statements about language minority students and language acquisition that recurred on a regular basis. These statements had a quality much like those of "urban legends"—that is, stories that are repeated around the country by word of mouth (or via the Internet), seemingly plausible, often mysterious, and inevitably false.

We realized that the education of language minority students in the United States also appeared to have a body of "myths" attached to it—myths that we had heard over and over again working with educators. We thought it might be helpful to set some of these myths straight, addressing them head on, much like we do when we are conducting training workshops.

We began this book by jotting down a list of myths we had heard frequently. We then asked several mainstream educators to add to our list. We winnowed the list down, organized it into several themes, and tried to provide a conversational discussion of the basic research that refutes the myths. We added a few vignettes to ground the research and provide a more realistic, day-to-day view of how things really operate in schools.

If you have ever thought that young children are better language learners than older children or that bilingual programs don't work, then this book is designed for you. You will probably find a few surprises here. We hope that the information will help you better serve the fastest growing group of students in the United States—language minority students. We also hope that the information presented here will help you to dispel these myths when you hear them recited in your school or community.

Chapter 1

Demographic Myths

Demographic Myth #1: The number of students who don't speak English is going down.

Reality: Language minority students, including limited English-proficient (LEP) students, are the fastest growing group of students in the United States today.

Background/Overview

Enrollment figures, as reported by State Education Agencies (SEAs) in the United States and its territories, have reflected an upward trend over the last several years. The most recent figures available for the 1993–1994 school year indicate a 16% increase over the 1992–1993 school year. Nearly 3,038,000 LEP students were enrolled in public or nonpublic elementary or secondary schools during the 1993–1994 school year, representing an increase of approximately 400,000 LEP students. For the period 1985 to 1994, the average yearly increase in the number of LEP students was 9.6%. The highest annual increase (17.5%) occurred between the 1987–1988 and 1988–1989 school years. All three states with the largest LEP student populations— California (1,215,000), Texas (422,700), and New York (216,400)—reported substantial increases in their LEP populations over the 1992–1993 school year.

According to a recent study, most LEP students are young (Fleischman & Hopstock 1993). More than two out of three are in grades K through 6, 18% are in grades 7 through 9, and 14% are in grades 10 through 12. The study also revealed that Spanish is the native language of approximately three out of four LEP students. Four percent speak Vietnamese, followed by Hmong, Cantonese, Cambodian, and Korean (2% each). One of twenty-nine different Native American languages is spoken by 2.5% of LEP students.

A further confirmation of this upward trend in the number of language minority students is seen in a recent article in *Education Week*. The article showed that as of July 1, 1998, the number of Hispanic children in the United States outnumbered African American children, making Hispanics the largest minority group among children younger than 18 years of age (Jacobson 1998).

1

Useful Resources for Statistical Information

Bureau of the Census, U.S. Department of Commerce, Census Data User Services Division, Washington DC 20033. For education information: (301) 457-2464.

National Center for Education Statistics, Office of Educational Research and Improvement, U.S. Department of Education, Education Information Branch, Capitol Place Building, Suite 300, 555 New Jersey Avenue NW, Washington DC 20208-5641. (800) 424-1616 or (202) 219-1651.

Numbers and Needs, ed. Dorothy Waggoner, Box GIH\B, 3900 Watson Place NW, Washington DC 20016. A newsletter that provides information from the Bureau of Census, the U.S. Department of Education, and other agencies to people concerned with the needs of the culturally and linguistically different.

Demographic Myth #2: Most limited English-proficient (LEP) students were born outside of the United States; most LEP students are recent arrivals to the United States.

Reality: Most LEP students were born here; only 20% of LEP students have been in the United States a year or less.

Background/Overview

Many LEP students are not immigrants or recent arrivals. A surprising number of students who are limited in English were born in the United States. As Fleischman and Hopstock (1993) demonstrate in Table 1–1, the percentage of LEP students born in the United States was highest in elementary school (almost 41%), but overall, the percentage of LEP students born in the United States is about one-third of the total number of LEP students. Most of these students were born into families in which languages other than English are regularly (and sometimes exclusively) spoken in the home (Fleischman & Hopstock 1993).

Demographic Myth #3: Students who do not speak English are found only in large, urban areas.

Reality: Students who do not speak English are found in many districts in the United States.

Background/Overview

A large-scale study commissioned by the Department of Education and published in 1993 found that approximately 6,400 of the 15,000 school districts in this country had LEP students enrolled, with the number varying from one student in some districts to as many as 242,000 in the Los Angeles Unified School District (Fleischman & Hopstock 1993). Table 1–2 shows the distribution of districts that served different

Table 1–1
Place of Birth and Length of U.S. Residence of LEP Students

MEAN PERCENTAGE OF LEP STUDENTS BY GRADE LEVEL					
Place of Birth/Length of U.S. Residence	Elementary	Middle	High	Multilevel	Total
Born in the United States	40.6	20.9	13.4	36.8	33.0
Born elsewhere but lived in the United States for at least five years	9.7	15.0	12.6	11.6	11.1
Born elsewhere but lived in the United States for one to four years	31.9	40.3	47.0	36.8	36.0
Born elsewhere but lived in the United States for less than one year	17.7	23.7	26.9	14.8	19.9
Total	100.0	100.0	100.0	100.0	100.0

(Source: Fleischman and Hopstock 1993)

numbers of LEP students. Approximately 24% of districts that served any LEP students served nine or fewer such students. On the other hand, 8% of districts served 1,000 or more LEP students. In terms of concentrations of LEP students, while almost half of the districts with LEP students served student populations that were less than 2% LEP, 6% of districts served a student population that was at least 40% LEP.

High concentrations of LEP and language minority students can generally be found in urban areas; LEP and language minority students are also found in suburban and rural districts. Table 1–3 (taken from the National Clearinghouse for Bilingual Education website) shows the school districts with the top ten LEP enrollments.

Demographic Myth #4: Only teachers in urban areas can expect to teach LEP students.

Reality: About 50% of teachers —one out of two— can expect to teach an LEP student sometime during their teaching careers.

Background/Overview

As early as 1980–1981, the Teachers Language Skills Survey (a study commissioned by the U.S. Department of Education) showed that an estimated one-half of all public school teachers in the United States reported that they were currently teaching (or had previously taught) LEP students (O'Malley & Waggoner 1984). Given the dramatic rise in the numbers of language minority and LEP students since that time, one can only assume that the percentage is higher today.

Table 1–2
Number of LEP Students Per District

NUMBER OF LEP STUDENTS	PERCENTAGE OF DISTRICTS
1–9	23.5
10–24	12.6
25–49	17.6
50–99	13.7
100–249	11.9
250–499	7.9
500–999	4.9
1,000–9,999	7.3
10,000 or more	0.6
Total	100.0

(Source: Fleischman & Hopstock 1993)

Although many LEP students spend most of their day in a regular classroom, regular classroom teachers often are unprepared to work with the LEP student effectively. Early on, Penfield (1987) explored the attitudes and perceptions of 162 regular classroom teachers regarding LEP students, English as a second language (ESL), and the role of ESL teachers. Analysis of the responses showed that many teachers felt unprepared to teach LEP students effectively and had little knowledge of how to integrate content teaching and English language development. In fact, the regular teachers felt it was the job of the ESL teacher to teach both academic subject matter and ESL— believing that ESL teachers spoke the native language of each student and even taught in this language.

Today, the situation has changed somewhat. In some states, such as Florida, *all* teachers must have some training that prepares them to work with LEP students (although what that training consists of is quite variable: from a single course, up to eighteen hours of course work depending on how many LEP students the district generally serves). Many teacher preparation programs (especially those that are accredited by the National Council of the Accreditation of Teacher Education [NCATE]) require graduating teachers to have some course work that speaks to the needs of LEP students. However, given the dramatic growth in the population of language minority students, it is difficult to tell if these measures will be enough in the years to come. The National Commission on Teaching and America's Future (NCTAF), which recently issued a series of recommendations for improving teacher quality, agrees: "Teachers need to understand how students of different language backgrounds and cultures can be supported in learning academic content and how those with a range of approaches to learning can be met with a variety of teaching strategies" (p.13).

Table 1–3
Local Education Agencies with Highest LEP Student Enrollment (1993–1994)

RANK	DISTRICT	NO. LEPS	TOTAL ENROLLMENT	% LEP
1	Los Angeles, CA	291,527	639,129	45.6%
2	New York, NY	154,526	1,015,756	15.2%
3	Chicago, IL	57,964	409,499	14.2%
4	Dade County, FL	54,735	422,658	13.0%
5	Houston, TX	50,839	200,839	25.3%
6	Santa Ana, CA	33,540	48,407	69.3%
7	San Diego, CA	33,397	127,258	26.2%
8	Dallas, TX	31,522	142,810	22.1%
9	Long Beach, CA	26,042	76,783	33.9%
10	Fresno, CA	24,022	76,349	31.5%
11	Garden Grove, CA	17,856	41,664	42.9%
12	San Francisco, CA	17,673	61,631	28.7%
13	El Paso, TX	17,609	64,145	27.5%
14	Montebello, CA	14,988	32,321	46.4%
15	Glendale, CA	14,930	28,742	51.9%
16	Broward County, FL	14,622	236,885	6.2%
17	Boston, MA	14,518	59,613	24.4%
18	Oakland, CA	14,044	51,748	27.1%
19	Pomona, CA	13,381	29,880	44.8%
20	Sacramento, CA	12,290	49,997	24.6%

(*Ask NCBE No. 2 – Which School Districts in the U.S. Have the Highest LEP Enrollment?* Reprinted with permission from the National Clearinghouse for Bilingual Education <http://www.ncbe.gwu.edu>)

Scenario

It is mid-April. Three preservice teachers, Deidre, Alva, and Michael, are having lunch together in the 25 minutes available between late afternoon and evening classes. They are talking about their heavy class load:

Deidre: *This program is just about killing me. I'm learning a lot, but I have no time for myself. Although what we're learning in our second language acquisition class is interesting, it's not at all useful to me. A couple of kids in my placement have Chinese names, but there's not a single LEP kid. What good is this second language acquisition class to me right now? Or in the future? My principal has already told me that they have a job for me, and that's where I'd like to work. I wish I could drop this class, just so I could have a bit more time for myself.*

Alva: *I know what you mean, because I'm teaching a class of African American kids. One hundred percent of them are African American. It just doesn't make sense to require that we all take this class.*

Michael: *I'm not sure I agree with you. Maybe that's because there are a few ESOL [English to Speakers of Other Languages] kids in my class, so it seems more relevant. But, how do you know you'll always teach English-speaking kids? I'm not sure any district is immune to immigration.*

Mid-April one year later: Deidre, Alva, and Michael are completing their first year as teachers. They see each other at a new teacher staff development day sponsored by the county office of education. Again, the conversation turns to nonnative English-speaking students:

Michael: *Do you remember last year how we talked about whether we needed our second language acquisition course? I've been wondering about you both. How's it going?*

Alva: *Well, I knew that being a first-year teacher would be difficult, but I wasn't expecting to be teaching LEP kids, also. Over the summer, my district decided to mix up the ethnic groups, I guess in some kind of a bid to get rid of segregation. So now I've got about a third of the class who speak a whole bunch of languages like Vietnamese, Portuguese, Croatian, and Farsi. It's been hard, and now I wish that I'd paid more attention to that course.*

Michael: *I have kids who speak nine different languages, and if it weren't for our ESOL teacher, I think I'd be in desperate shape. But, she comes into my class every day and helps me out. I've gone back to our course reader over and over again. I'd have been lost completely without that course.*

Deidre: *It's still the same for me. Only English speakers. Though there's talk of some families from Central America moving into the district. I heard that a local nursery has been hiring men from Central America and now they're bringing in their families. But I don't think that it'll affect me as my school is in a pretty high-income area.*

Mid-April two years later: It is a Saturday, and Deidre, Alva, and Michael are chatting together over coffee at a one-day institute on science and second language learners sponsored by a local technical assistance center:

Alva: *What on earth are you doing here, Deidre? I thought your school was an English-only school.*

Deidre: *It was, but not any more. A lot of kids from El Salvador and Guatemala have moved into the district, and our school has been designated as the site for the newcomer students. They spend half the day in a class for just newcomers, but then they spend the rest of the day with the rest of us. Plus, a local church is sponsoring refugees from Eastern Europe—Bosnia, I think.*

Michael: *So, does everyone have ESOL kids?*

Deidre: *Just about everyone, though the upper grade teachers don't have as many right now. The irony is that my principal was thrilled that I had taken those second language acquisition courses and had the supplemental credential. I didn't like to disappoint him and tell him that I hadn't paid much attention. To be honest, though, a lot of what we learned in the program is coming back, so maybe I wasn't as zoned out as I thought! It's hard, though, particularly as I haven't seen any good teachers who have experience working with second language learners. I'm lucky, though, because my principal is really supportive of us and we get materials and as much staff development as we want. And to think I had it all figured out!*

Chapter 2

Enrollment Myths

Enrollment Myth #1: School districts are not obliged to enroll students who are not legal residents of the United States.

Reality: The federal government mandates that states provide equal public education for undocumented immigrant children.

Background/Overview

In 1982, the Supreme Court ruled in *Plyler v. Doe*, 457 U.S. 202, that public schools were prohibited from denying immigrant students access to a public education from kindergarten to grade 12 on the basis of their immigrant status. More specifically, under the Equal Protection Clause of the Fourteenth Amendment to the Constitution, states and public schools are barred from denying undocumented students their right of access to public schools on the basis of their legal status. In essence, the Supreme Court has held their right of access to be a semi-fundamental right, which can only be violated if the state can show that disparate treatment promotes a substantial state interest (Carrera 1989).

The Supreme Court stated that under current laws and practices, "the illegal alien of today may well be the legal alien of tomorrow," and that without an education, these undocumented children, already disadvantaged as a result of poverty, lack of English-speaking ability, and undeniable racial prejudices, will become permanently locked into the lowest socioeconomic class. Thus, the Court found that undocumented children and young adults have the same right to attend free public primary and secondary schools as their U.S. citizen and permanent resident peers. In addition to the right of access conveyed by *Plyler*, both documented and undocumented immigrant students are obligated, as are all other students, to attend primary and secondary schools until they reach a mandated age.

Enrollment Myth # 2: School districts are allowed to charge tuition of students who are not legal residents of the United States.

Reality: Public schools cannot charge tuition of any student who meets the standard residency requirements of that district.

Background/Overview

Under constitutional state residency requirements, all school-age children, including immigrant students, must be deemed as residents if they or their parent or legal guardian live in the district with a bona fide intention of remaining there. The phrase *intention to remain* does not imply an intention never to leave. Given the mobility of people in this country, changing a place of residence is commonplace. Under *Plyler v. Doe*, 457 U.S. 202 (1982), the distinction between undocumented persons, on the one hand, and documented persons and U.S. citizens, on the other, does not constitute a bona fide residency requirement (Carrera 1989). Thus, immigrant students residing in the United States cannot be denied resident status by public schools solely on the basis of their nonimmigrant status.

Although the Supreme Court has never ruled on the issue, a lower court (*Peña v. Board of Education of City of Atlanta*, 620 F. Supp. 293, 1985) ruled that the Fourteenth Amendment Equal Protection Clause was violated when the plaintiff, a local school district, required that tuition be paid for public school admission of the children of certain nonimmigrant parents (such as those here on visas such as the B-2 [temporary visitor for pleasure]), but not for all nonimmigrant parents, such as diplomats or journalists. We can therefore conclude that all foreign-born students residing here as dependents of parents or guardians who are here on nonimmigrant visas have the same right of access to a free primary and secondary public education as that enjoyed by citizens and undocumented students.

Enrollment Myth #3: Schools should ask for proof of citizenship, resident visas, or Social Security numbers when enrolling second language (L2) students.

Reality: Schools are prohibited from asking for documentation of a student's legal status.

Background/Overview

Requests for information such as a visa, proof of citizenship, or Social Security number may have a "chilling" effect on students' legal right of access to a free primary or secondary public education. Therefore, inquiring about a student's immigration status and making inquiries that might expose the undocumented status of a student or her parents during initial enrollment (or at any other time) are practices that are prohibited under the Supreme Court decision, *Plyler v. Doe*, 457 U.S. 202 (1982). Likewise, since undocumented students and undocumented parents are not eligible for Social Security numbers, any school that requires Social Security numbers as a prerequisite for enrollment would be denying all undocumented students the right of access in direct violation of *Plyler v. Doe.*

Should the school come across information regarding the immigration status of students or their parents, it is prohibited under the Family Educational Rights and Privacy Act (FERPA) from providing any outside agency (including the Immigration and Naturalization Service [INS]) with all such information. School personnel should be prohibited from cooperating with INS in any manner that jeopardizes or could jeopardize immigrant students' legal right of access under *Plyler v. Doe* (Carrera 1989).

Scenario

School ended over two hours ago, the hallways at Wilson Middle School are now quiet, and the principal, Jessica Lee, and assistant principal, Pat Davis, are chatting over a cup of coffee:

Jessica Lee: Can you believe what the school board voted to do last night?

Pat Davis: You mean now having to check whether students who speak a language other than English are here legally? (Jessica nods). I thought it was a bit odd, didn't you?

Jessica Lee: Not just odd, but downright evil-spirited. Can you imagine how our families who don't speak much English are going to feel? I feel as if all the effort we've put into welcoming our ESOL kids and their families is going down the drain. It makes me so mad to think that now we're going to have to be immigration officials. If I'd wanted to do that, I wouldn't have entered teaching. (Pause) It doesn't feel right to me. It's almost as if they're telling us that all the great things we've done to help our newcomer students feel at home and succeed have been totally ignored. And they say it's a budget concern. What about the students whose parents are from Ireland and England and Australia? How come we're not required to ask them for proof of residency? Interesting how it's only the kids who aren't native English speakers. Oh, I don't know why I said that, as I don't think we should be asking anyone for that kind of ID.

Pat Davis: You know, when I got home last night, I was talking with a friend about the board's decision and he said something about it being illegal. I didn't pay much attention then, but I think I'll give him a call and see what he knows. He works with an immigration rights organization in the city.

The next day, Jessica and Pat meet before school. Pat is carrying a piece of paper.

Pat Davis: Look at this. I saw my friend last night, and guess what? It is illegal to require documentation. It's something to do with a U.S. Supreme Court case in 1982. Here it is. Plyler v. Doe. Look, the Supreme Court ruled that "undocumented children and young adults have the same right to attend public primary and secondary schools as do U.S. citizens and permanent residents. Like other children, undocumented students are required under state laws to attend school until they reach a legally mandated age." So, presumably, the board could be sued if they insist on us asking for immigration documentation.

Jessica Lee: Yes, you're probably right. It's the first I've heard of this case. I wonder why they never mentioned it in my school law course when I was in the administration program? This is very interesting. Where did your friend get this document, do you know?

Pat Davis: Actually, while I was there, he went on the Internet and showed me this web site for an organization called NCAS. That stands for something like National Coalition of Advocates for Students. They have a Clearinghouse for Immigrant Education and this "alert" is one of the things they do. It looked pretty interesting and useful.

Jessica Lee: I think I'll look into it later on today. Right now, though, I'm going to make a copy of this "alert" and send it over to central office. That should get things moving.

Chapter 3

Native Language (L1)
Instruction Myths

L1 Instruction Myth #1: Teachers in English medium classrooms should not allow students to use their native language, as this will retard their English language development.

Reality: Allowing students to use their native language facilitates cognitive and academic growth.

Background/Overview

Imagine yourself sitting in a classroom in St. Petersburg. The teacher is moving everyone into groups to begin a hands-on science lesson about photosynthesis. You are expected to work in groups, performing several experiments with plants. The process requires you to plant, measure, discuss, evaluate results, and prepare a report. Now imagine that the classroom you're in is located in St. Petersburg, Russia, instead of St. Petersburg, Florida. Other than you and one other student, all the other students are native speakers of Russian. You have had an introductory Russian course, but you are still limited Russian proficient. You have, however, studied photosynthesis in your old school in the United States, so you know the science. How do you cope with the assignments and activities you've been given?

Now imagine that you had not been previously taught the concepts of photosynthesis in English. Would you need to adopt new strategies to complete the assignment? If you've never studied the concept of photosynthesis, the cognitive and linguistic burden placed on you is much heavier than that of your native Russian-speaking peers because you will have to gain access to new scientific concepts and vocabulary through a language you do not speak, read, or write well (McKeon 1994). If you were being judged on your ability to do the science, do you think that having access to materials in English would help? Would it help if your teacher (who has a working knowledge of English) could supply a few key phrases or translate a few critical concepts for you? Would performing the experiments and discussing the results with your one English-speaking classmate help you figure out the concepts? You bet they would! Would the fact that you had done all this in English impair your ability to learn Russian? Not a chance.

Yet when we view this same problem through the lens of LEP students in the United States, most teachers and administrators find a host of reasons why having students use their native language is wrong or undesirable. In fact, the research on bilingualism supports the notion that cognitive and academic skills such as those described in the foregoing example transfer from one language to another (Hakuta 1986; Handscombe 1994). In addition, the research suggests that providing students with substantial amounts of instruction in their native language does *not* interfere with or delay their acquisition of English language skills (Ramirez 1991).

L1 Instruction Myth #2: Bilingual education is a luxury we cannot afford.

Reality: The actual cost of bilingual education is largely unknown; however, whatever the cost, it may be worth it in terms of the benefits.

Background/Overview

To date, there have been painfully few studies that examine the cost of bilingual education (Prince & Hubert 1994). Sorting out "differential costs"—the costs which are above and beyond what would normally be required in the district's program for speakers of English (i.e., those costs that make up the difference between basic instructional costs and the total costs of educating students in bilingual education programs) is not an easy task. Bilingual education poses additional problems for cost analysts because the determination of what constitutes a differential cost tends to vary by program type. For example, the salary of a teacher in a self-contained bilingual education class, who is responsible for all classroom instruction (i.e., native language, English language, and content area instruction), would not be considered a differential cost because a teacher would still be needed if all of the students in the class were proficient in English. By contrast, the salary of a resource teacher who provides supplementary native language or ESOL instruction to small groups of students for a portion of the day would be considered a differential cost, since resource teachers are hired in addition to regular classroom teachers (Prince & Hubert 1994).

These difficulties notwithstanding, one recent examination of the differential cost of bilingual education in Hartford, Connecticut, showed that differential costs were found to be about $680 per pupil, or only about 15% of the per-pupil costs in Hartford.

On the other side of the coin, *not* providing bilingual education can be costly in human terms. Take the dropout rate. Twenty to thirty percent of Hispanic young adults are classified as dropouts, compared with 8.6% for non-Hispanic whites and 12.1% for non-Hispanic blacks (Krashen 1998).

There is some evidence showing that bilingual education actually results in lower dropout rates for Hispanic students who are LEP. Krashen (1998) points to a study that compared dropout rates for students who had one or more years of bilingual education with those from a similar group who had not had bilingual education. The bilingually educated group of students had a significantly lower dropout rate.

Finally, the economic benefits of producing truly bilingual citizens may far outweigh any programmatic costs incurred. A new study by Boswell (1998), examining the Hispanic population in Florida, shows that there is a clear and consistent tendency for Florida's Hispanics who speak English very well, in addition to speaking Spanish, to have higher incomes than those Hispanics who speak only English. People who speak English very well and who also speak Spanish have annual median and mean incomes that are about $2,000 higher than for Hispanics who speak only English. Boswell notes that the advantage gained by knowing both Spanish and English is lost if a person does not speak English very well. In this case, the lower English proficiency counteracts the advantage of knowing Spanish. Clearly though, the economic benefits of being truly bilingual are suggested by this work.

L1 Instruction Myth #3: When LEP students speak in their native language in English medium classes, they are likely to be off-task.

Reality: Such students are about as likely to be off-task as monolingual English speakers.

Background/Overview

There is no question that monolingual English-speaking teachers often find the non-English language discussions of students distracting and somewhat suspicious—particularly if students seem to be laughing at the same time they are talking. These teachers have no way of knowing what students are talking about, a fact that some students may relish and make the most of. However, most of the time in class, speakers of other languages may need to confer with one another to check meaning, ask for help, or let off the pressure of being schooled for 6 or 7 hours a day in a language in which they are not proficient.

The reaction of teachers is understandable, however. It is difficult for teachers to feel that they are not communicating well with students—or that students are not communicating well with them. One of the things we often do in workshops to help teachers understand this phenomenon better is to teach a "shock" language lesson. That is, we start off delivering the workshop completely in Spanish. We then administer a test in Spanish. Most of the time, there are one or two folks in the group who either speak Spanish well or who have taken enough Spanish in school to piece together a bit of what's going on. Immediately, those folks become the "leaders" for the others, who turn to them for help in understanding what we're saying. After about 15 minutes of this (it really doesn't take long), when participants are getting frustrated, we call a halt to the shock lesson and debrief the group. One of the things we ask the participants to examine is the strategies they used to cope with the new language and the classroom demands being placed on them. Invariably, they describe talking with one of the "leaders," asking them for information and guidance, trying to figure out how to complete the task. Participants generally come to the realization that their behavior mirrors that of their students.

Activities of this sort can go a long way in helping monolingual teachers understand and be more tolerant of student behavior that they might otherwise view as objectionable. We also find that once teachers can get past the awkwardness of having students speak in a language they don't understand, the teachers can learn to become adept at knowing when students are on- or off-task, regardless of the language students are using.

Scenario

Sam Atang is accustomed to having visitors join his third grade class, particularly before lunch during writers' workshop. He is a district writing mentor and is considered one of the best writing teachers in the region. Today, he quickly greets a friend from a neighboring school, Judy Olsen-Diaz, who has just entered the classroom, and invites her to join the class on the blue rug for the day's minilesson. Judy follows him and sits on the outskirts of the double semicircle of students, where she can easily hear and observe the class.

The minilesson is about embarrassing moments, and Sam begins by remarking that he has been reading some pieces that seem to be very personal, maybe embarrassing for the writers and their families. Soon after Sam says "embarrassing," Javier giggles and turns to his neighbor, Ernesto. The two boys begin talking together in Spanish in low voices. Sam waits for a couple of seconds, and then reminds the boys that they need to listen and show respectful behavior. He continues with his minilesson: "We've been talking about how it's often easier to write about people and events that we know well. I just want to make sure that everyone understands that writers don't have to reveal everything about themselves to their audiences. You're entitled to keep some things private." He glances over at Javier and Ernesto, who are once again engaging in a whispered conversation in Spanish. Sam waits, and when he sharply calls out their names, the two boys stop talking.

At the end of the minilesson, the children move to clusters of desks, where they open up their writing folders and begin writing, reading, revising, conferring, and illustrating their books. Judy is a Spanish-English bilingual teacher and decides to shadow Javier and Ernesto. She notices that they use Spanish almost exclusively when talking together. She notices that almost all of their conversation is related to the task at hand (e.g., Ernesto telling Javier how to spell English words or explaining what to do next). She notices that Ernesto appears to be bilingual and acts as a translator for Javier and the English-speaking children. For example, when Jennifer points to Javier's writing and accompanying drawing of a boat capsizing and asks what happened, Ernesto questions Javier in Spanish and conveys Javier's response to Jennifer in English: "The boat sank." Ernesto is writing a bilingual version of a book about baseball, and Judy notices that when the two boys confer on the book, it is very much a collaboration, with Javier sometimes correcting Ernesto's Spanish writing.

At the end of the morning, when Sam and Judy have time to debrief, they talk about Javier and Ernesto:

Sam: Although I've been teaching for a while, these two boys stretch me the most.

Judy: Why's that?

Sam: Well, you saw them today. They're always chattering away together, and most of the time, no, all of the time, it's in Spanish. I normally don't have that kind of problem with students, but I'm ready to separate them.

Judy: I don't think I'd do that, though I can see how it might be a bit distracting when you're talking and they're talking at the same time. I decided to shadow them this morning, and what struck me was that almost all of their conversations were about their writing. And you're right, they were all in Spanish, though Javier used an occasional English word. Also, Ernesto was doing a wonderful job of helping Javier talk with the kids who don't speak Spanish. Basically, he was a translator for the group.

Sam: Really? I would never have guessed that. I guess I need to observe more closely and touch base with them more often. But, you know, sometimes they seem a bit disrespectful. Like this morning, when Javier laughed out loud when I was doing the minilesson on writing about embarrassing things.

Judy: I couldn't hear everything that they were saying then, but I heard Ernesto telling Javier that it had nothing to do with being pregnant.

Sam: Pregnant?! What's that got to do with being embarrassed?

Judy: Well, in Spanish, the word for being pregnant is "embarasada," which sounds an awful lot like embarrassed, doesn't it?! I wondered if Javier had laughed because he thought you had said someone was pregnant.

Sam: Oh, no, now I feel like a complete fool. I need to talk with the boys. Maybe I also need to make more of Ernesto's ability to speak two languages. I noticed that he was writing his book in both languages, which is a first in my experience. I wonder why he decided to do that? I need to find out. And I need to make sure that we celebrate it. This just goes to show that we never stop learning! Thanks for all your help.

Chapter 4

Myths About Acquiring a Second Language (L2)

Second Language Acquisition Myth #1: Learning a second language is an entirely different proposition from learning one's own native language.

Reality: There are many parallels between learning a first and second language.

Background/Overview

It may be comforting for educators to know that learning the linguistic structures and rules of a second language occurs in much the same way as it does for the first (Dulay, Burt & Krashen 1982; Lindfors 1989). In fact, if we think of language as a coin, we can think of first and second language learning as its two sides: essentially the same in composition, but with different designs and different features.

Whether first or second language learning, people learn language because they are in real situations communicating about important and interesting things. Furthermore, this communication is seen and perceived as something that is highly valued (Urzúa 1989). An initial look at the environments in which young children develop their language reveals a great deal of linguistic variety, yet virtually all children effortlessly and naturally learn their native tongues. Children's first language development before they come to school takes place largely through conversations that they hear and have with members of their families.

At one time, it was thought that children learned language by imitating their parents. More recent research suggests, however, that children learn language by actively constructing principles for the regularities that they hear in the speech of others, such as parents, brothers and sisters, and those they interact with on a regular basis (Brown 1973; Chomsky 1969). Evidence of these principles can be seen when children use forms such as *goed*, (as in, "My daddy goed to the store yesterday"), *foots*, and even *feets*. Such errors in children's speech provide us with clues that children are indeed constructing their own hypotheses of how the language functions, since they haven't heard these particular forms in the speech of adults (Wells 1986). As language develops, children become capable of dealing with greater degrees of complexity. They

17

begin to recognize the inconsistencies of their own speech. They modify their hypotheses about the rules of language and gradually reorganize their language system so that their language approximates more complex adult forms—*goed* becomes *went*.

Learners who are acquiring a second language typically "try out" the language with equal creative fervor, making errors that are similar to the errors made by young monolingual speakers of the language. These errors are an integral part of the second language learning process, helping learners to refine and revise their understanding of how the second language works. Beginning learners of English as a second language (ESL), regardless of age, are as likely to say *goed* and *foots* as first language learners of English, suggesting that learners gradually organize the language they hear according to rules they construct in the new language. Gradually, as the learner's language system develops, these rules are refined to incorporate more and more of the language system.

Second language learners, like children who are acquiring their first language, often appear to understand language before being able to produce it (Dulay, Burt & Krashen 1982). In fact, many children who are acquiring a second langauge have been observed to exhibit a "silent period," saying nothing (or very little) in the new language being learned for periods ranging from several days to several months. For schools and teachers, these features of second language acquisition are often a source of confusion and concern about a child's learning abilities. It may be reassuring to know, therefore, that these silent periods are considered to be a natural part of second language acquisition, have no long-term detrimental effect on language learning overall, and may, in fact, be beneficial to the second language learning process, providing learners with time to hypothesize about the rules of the new language they are learning.

Although first and second language acquisition are similar processes in many ways, they are by no means identical. Second language learners are more sophisticated learners, in that they already have acquired some, if not most, of the components of one language. Second language learners are more cognitively mature than are first language learners (unless, of course, they are acquiring two languages from birth). See Figure 4–1 for features of L2 Acquisition.

Scenario

It is just before Thanksgiving, and the students in Raúl Castro's kindergarten class are preparing to make construction paper turkeys, complete with multicolored tails. For the first time, Mr. Castro's class includes several students whose parents speak a language other than English at home. One of these students, Mee Lon, has Mr. Castro worried. She seems to understand what's going on in class and is a willing participant in activities such as the one going on today, but Mee Lon rarely, if ever, speaks. Mr. Castro decides to consult with Karen Kelly, Mee Lon's ESL teacher.

Raúl Castro: Karen, I just don't understand what's going on with Mee Lon. She's really got me wondering if I should refer her for Special Education testing. She never speaks in class, although she seems to be following along with what we're doing— much better than she did at the beginning of the year—and is fairly outgoing with her peers. But even with the other children, she almost never says anything.

Figure 4–1
Features of L2 Acquisition

- L1 and L2 acquisition are similar processes, *but*
  - L2 learners are more cognitively mature than L1 learners
- Language learning involves hypothesis construction and testing:
  - Errors are integral to language learning
- Understanding language usually precedes language production
  - A "silent period" is normal
- Younger learners do not necessarily have greater facility with languages:
  - Older learners generally confront more complex linguistic situations
  - Younger learners may pronounce the L2 with minimal accent, *but*
  - Older learners are often more efficient learners
- Mastering academic language may take L2 learners up to 7 years
- L2 acquisition and academic success are influenced by sociocultural factors, e.g.,
  - Personality
  - Cultural affiliation
  - Prior schooling
  - Teacher expectations

Karen: I know. She's that way in ESL class, too. And you can imagine how frustrating it is for me when we do oral work—telling stories and playing games. But, you know I recently reread something about a phenomenon called "the silent period." It occurs sometimes when kids are learning another language. Even though they may be listening to and processing what's going on around them, they just don't speak—at least not in the beginning.

Raúl: But it's almost Thanksgiving! And Mee Lon has been in school since late August.

Karen: I know, but sometimes that's how long it takes. Sometimes, even longer. I asked our family outreach worker to check with Mee Lon's parents to see if she's that way at home. They said that when she's home playing with her brothers, she's a regular motor-mouth in Mandarin. I guess it must be pretty intimidating to be placed in a school where everything is happening in a language you don't understand—and plus, the fact that this is her first school experience must be contributing to her shyness.

Raúl: So what did your book say about dealing with this? Can I ever hope to hear a peep out of her? Won't this delay her development in English?

Karen: Actually, what I read suggested that this "silent period" won't hurt her development in any way. If you can find activities that she can participate in by drawing or pointing, that will help you know that she's understanding. Also, if you can get her to join in to games or songs where others are talking or singing at the same time, that might alleviate some of the pressure on her to give a "solo" performance. You know, the book said that some adults have been known to go through this "silent period," too. I plan to hang on, be patient, and give her a chance to work it out. Although I read that a silent period can last up to 6 months, I bet she'll be talking by Christmas. If she's this into the turkeys, imagine when we get to the reindeer!

Second Language Acquisition Myth #2: Younger children are more effective language learners than are older learners.

Reality: While younger language learners may learn to pronounce a new language with little or no accent, older language learners are often more efficient learners.

Background/Overview

Although it has long been thought that young children are more effective language learners, there is some evidence to suggest that this is not the case, except for a greater facility with pronunciation (Dulay, Burt & Krashen 1982). What leads people to imagine that young children are expert linguists is the fact that the types of linguistic tasks young children are expected to perform are generally simple face-to-face communicative activities that fit their developmental level. With increasing age, the language (including the written form of the language) that students must comprehend and use to match their developmental level rapidly outstrips their rudimentary command of the second language, thus creating a mismatch (if not a tremendous chasm) between conceptual and linguistic competence.

The mismatch between conceptual and linguistic competence is often seen most starkly in school settings. Older school-age learners require more sophisticated language skills, which help them maneuver through complex social situations and challenging academic situations. Language researchers and theoreticians have recently begun to explore the ways in which these more complex forms of language vary and, in turn, how that variation affects the ability of students to learn and use language in academic settings (Bialystok 1991; Collier 1987, 1989; Chamot and O'Malley 1985; Crandall 1987; Cummins 1981b; Mohan 1986). The context in which language is used and the conceptual content of communication are two possible sources of variation that have been explored.

Differences in the context in which language is used also help to account for some of the reasons why younger children may be seen as better language learners. The context of language use refers to the degree to which the environment is rich with meaningful clues that help the language learner decipher and interpret the language being used. Face-to-face conversations, for example, provide the opportunity to observe nonverbal cues such as facial expressions and gestures. Tone of voice conveys meaning far beyond what mere words can express, as any child listening to a frustrated parent demand that toys be picked up *now* can attest.

Children learning to play a game not only have the verbal directions to rely on in helping them figure out the game, but also can actually watch others playing. Language used in environments that contain plentiful clues to meaning is described as context-embedded (Cummins 1981a, 1981b), and these environments are generally thought to be "easier" for learners to navigate. Context-embedded or contextualized language use is evident in some types of school activities, as well. In a science demonstration, for example, as the teacher explains the steps in performing an experiment, students can actually watch the actions, tying the language to something in "the here and now."

Decontextualized or context-reduced language use, on the other hand, occurs in environments that provide few meaningful clues to the learner. There is little in the immediate environment (other than the language itself) that will help learners derive meaning from the language being used, and it is thus seen as "harder" for second language learners. Oral language that is decontextualized can be exemplified by telephone conversations, when a listener no longer can rely on facial expressions or gestures to infer meaning. Reading (especially in books with no pictures) requires that the learner depend strictly on the message conveyed through the words on the page. Lectures (such as those often given in the upper elementary grades, middle school, and high school) that deal with topics such as the American Revolution or the greenhouse effect, provide little in the way of nonlinguistic clues to support meaning.

For children who are learning English as a second language, the implications of such language variation are significant. While children may be able to deduce meaning from context-embedded language, the process of understanding and mastering decontextualized language use is much more difficult. Since much of school language once one moves beyond the earliest grades tends to be decontextualized, children learning English as a second language in school often find themselves lost in a world of meaningless words.

Second Language Acquisition Myth #3: Once second language learners are able to speak reasonably fluently, their problems are likely to be over in school.

Reality: The ability to speak a second language (especially in conversational settings) does not guarantee that a student will be able to use the language effectively in academic settings.

Background/Overview

Do you remember what it was like to take a foreign language? You struggled with pronunciation and vocabulary, the conjugation of verb forms eluded you, the fight to make nouns and verbs (not to mention articles) agree seemed futile, your reading slowed to a snail's pace of translating word by painful word, and as your frustration level grew, you probably wondered, "Is it *really* worth it?" Now imagine the burden of having to cope with content area instruction in a subject like geometry or earth science at the same time. This is the challenge that LEP students face in school every day.

The content of communication—that is, what the language is about or relates to—is another variation that determines whether language is "easy" or "hard." Variation in content can result in different levels of cognitive demand on learners. Language used to communicate about objects and concrete concepts tends to place less of a cognitive load on learners than does language about complex notions or abstract ideas. Language that expresses what one already knows and understands is less cognitively demanding than that which teaches a new concept or principle.

In addition, researchers are now beginning to suggest that specific content domains (such as math, science, and history) are associated with specific varieties of language (Dale & Cuevas 1987; Kessler & Quinn 1987; King et al. 1987). The use of distinctive words, structures, and communicative functions has been found to vary with the particular content area being taught (e.g., the word *cabinet*, learned in a general context, refers to a cupboard; *cabinet* takes on a very different meaning in a social studies context, when used to refer to a group of presidential advisors).

It has been shown that school language becomes more complex and less contextualized in successively higher grades (Collier 1989; Cummins & Swain 1986). Thus, the ability to learn content area material becomes increasingly dependent on interaction with and mastery of the language connected to such material. The ability to demonstrate what one has learned also increasingly requires extensive use of oral and written forms of language. The academic consequences of such increased language demands on students are readily apparent. Careful planning of instruction is needed in order to help LEP students develop the decontextualized language skills they will need to master the cognitively demanding content in the higher grades.

Second Language Acquisition Myth #4: Learning academic English is equally challenging for all second language learners.

Reality: The challenge of learning English for school varies tremendously from learner to learner and depends on many factors.

Background/Overview

Discussions of language learning in an academic environment must also take into account students' previous exposure to content in their first language. Studies show that children who have had formal academic preparation in a given content area in their first language usually make greater progress initially in academic content in the second language (Collier 1989; Cummins 1981b). Unfortunately, some of the children entering U.S. schools today are students who lack even basic academic skills in the first language; many come from countries torn by war or civil unrest and have seldom, if ever, seen the inside of a classroom. Some may be illiterate in their first language or come from a language background that does not have a written form. It is clear that for such students, learning English in an academic setting will be a much more challenging task than for their counterparts who have received adequate schooling and who are literate and performing on grade level in their first language.

Second Language Acquisition Myth #5: If we focus on teaching the English language, learning in all areas will occur faster.

Reality: Language learning is a developmental process; while learning a language will not occur in the absence of exposure to the language, increased exposure to the language (particularly in academic settings) does not guarantee quicker learning.

Background/Overview

For schools, the bottom line of all the research on second language acquisition is probably embodied in the question, "How long does it take?" The answer is, "It depends." This answer is often seen as an unsatisfactory one by policymakers, in particular, who may try to legislate English language acquisition. The passage of California's Proposition 227 (also known as the Unz amendment), requiring that students be schooled exclusively in English, is an unfortunate case in point.

The fact is that the rate of second language acquisition (particularly in academic settings) is really a function of several variables. The age of students at the time of initial exposure to the second language, previous schooling in the first language, and the type of instruction provided in the second language—all influence the rate of L2 acquisition. Collier's (1989) synthesis of research on academic achievement in a second language offers the following generalizations drawn from an exhaustive review of the literature:

1. When students are schooled in two languages, with solid cognitive academic instruction provided in both the first and second language, they usually take from 4 to 7 years to reach national norms on standardized tests in reading, social studies and science, whereas their performance may reach national norms in as little as two years in mathematics and language arts (when the skills being tested include spelling, punctuation, and simple grammar points).

2. Immigrants arriving at ages 8 to 12, with at least 2 years of schooling in their first language, take 5 to 7 years to reach the level of average performance by native speakers of English on standardized tests in reading, social studies and science when they are schooled exclusively in English after arrival. Their performance may reach national norms in as little as 2 years in mathematics and language arts.

3. Young arrivals with no schooling in their first language may take as long as 7 to 10 years to reach the average level of performance of native English speakers on standardized tests in reading, social studies and science.

4. Adolescent arrivals with no previous exposure to the second language who are not provided with an opportunity to continue academic work in their first language do not have enough time left in high school to make up the lost years of academic instruction. This is true both for adolescents with a good academic background and for those whose schooling has been limited or interrupted.

5. Consistent, uninterrupted cognitive academic development in all subjects throughout students' schooling is more important than the number of hours of instruction in the second language for successful academic achievement in the second language.

The generalizations drawn by Collier (1989) point out the complex nature of second language acquisition in an academic environment. They also help to explain why some LEP students seem to perform better than others. The variety of factors that influence a student's ability to master challenging subject matter while acquiring another language (proficiency in the first language, ability to read and write in the first language, and previous schooling in the first language) also help to point out one inescapable fact that seems to have eluded many school districts: Just learning English will not guarantee a student's academic success.

The length of time that LEP students appear to need in order to master language for academic purposes accounts for some of the confusion experienced by teachers working with such learners. Many LEP children puzzle their teachers with displays of relatively proficient English in social settings such as the playground and the cafeteria, where contextualized language skills are sufficient. When these students move back into the classroom, however, their teachers are sometimes heard to say, "I think he knows more than he's letting on. I hear him using English on the playground, and yet when it's time to do social studies, his English suddenly disappears. Is he trying to fool me into thinking that he doesn't understand so that he can get out of work?" Probably not. In other words, in many cases, children who have achieved modest levels of contextualized English proficiency find themselves "mainstreamed" or exited from support programs that are needed to help them continue the process of acquiring the decontextualized language skills they need to cope with higher order concepts that are language dependent. The disparity between children's linguistic capabilities in social settings compared with their capabilities in academic settings often results in children being asked to handle a larger linguistic load than they are ready to carry, thus falling behind in the "regular" classes in which they've been placed.

Second Language Acquisition Myth #6: Students from Asian countries are better English language learners and more academically successful than students from Spanish-speaking backgrounds.

Reality: Students from all language and cultural backgrounds are equally capable of learning English as a second language; academic success cannot be attributed to language or cultural background, but rather to a variety of social, emotional, intellectual, and academic factors.

Background/Overview

No discussion of language minority and LEP children would be complete without some mention of the relationship of academic performance to cultural affiliation. Scholars have long documented cultural differences that exist between students' homes and the school (Guthrie 1985; Heath 1983, 1986; Ogbu 1992; Scarcella 1989), suggesting that there are discontinuities that exist for many groups who are not part of the "mainstream middle class." While such discontinuities may create hardships for all groups, some groups clearly seem to experience more difficulty in making the transition from home to school than do others. This is particularly true for language minority students. Many educators have observed that some language minority students seem to perform better in U.S. schools than do others, and they point to Asian "whiz-kids" who top out on the SATs and win science fairs.

Ogbu and Matute-Bianchi (1986) have examined variability in the school performance of different linguistic minority groups around the world. While the specific linguistic minority groups that do well in school vary from country to country, each country appears to achieve success in schooling some groups, while other groups languish. In addition, there appears to be evidence that variability in performance is affected by the country in which a particular group finds itself. Such a group may do well in one country, but poorly in another. One example of such variable performance is the case of Korean students, who have been shown to perform quite poorly in schools in Japan, while doing quite well in schools in the United States (DeVos & Lee 1981).

Researchers speculate that variability in the performance of linguistic minority students may be partly explained by examining the connection between education and other societal institutions and events affecting minorities (Cummins 1989; Matute-Bianchi 1986; Ogbu & Matute-Bianchi 1986; Ogbu 1992). In addition, they suggest that the social perceptions and experiences of particular minority groups can affect the outcome of their children's schooling. Immigrant minorities and "castelike" or indigenous minorities are two of the categories of minority groups that have been described (Ogbu & Matute-Bianchi 1986; Ogbu 1992; Ovando & Collier 1985). Let us say at the outset that it is important not to stereotype the behavior of any individual according to the categories, since within each category there is a wide range of adaptations to life in a given culture, and the designation of a particular group may change over time or in a particular context. The categories do help, however, to build a framework in which minority achievement can be better understood.

Immigrant minorities include groups that have moved more or less voluntarily to their new country for political, social, or economic reasons. Examples of such minorities in the United States are the Koreans (mentioned earlier), Japanese Americans,

Cuban Americans, and Chinese Americans. Immigrants in the immigrant minority category tend not to evaluate their success in the new country by comparing themselves with elite members of the host society; their frame of reference is still in the country from which they emigrated. They compare themselves either with their peers in the "old country" or with peers in the immigrant community.

Education is an important investment for such immigrant groups because it is perceived as the key to advancement, particularly for their children. Immigrant children are taught to accept schools' rules for behavior and achievement; they learn to switch back and forth between two cultural frames of reference—that of the home and that of the school. Their ability to make these adjustments without feeling that they are losing their own culture enhances their ability to perform effectively in school.

Caste-like or indigenous minorities are minorities that have become incorporated into a society more or less permanently and involuntarily (through such processes as conquest, colonization, and slavery), then relegated to a menial status within the larger group (Ogbu & Matute-Bianchi 1986). For example, Koreans (mentioned earlier) who were originally sent to Japan as colonial subjects in forced labor, perform poorly in school there and function as a caste-like minority in that setting. Mexican Americans, Native Americans, and Puerto Ricans may be examples of such minority groups in the United States.

Caste-like minorities tend to believe that they cannot advance into the mainstream of society through individual efforts in school or by adopting the cultural beliefs and practices of the dominant group. As Ovando and Collier (1985, 270) point out, "There is a tendency in the United States for mainstream whites to perceive indigenous minorities as being non-American, even if they have been here for generations." The belief that they cannot make it leads these minorities to adopt survival strategies to cope with the conditions in which they find themselves and to make them distinct from the dominant group. Such strategies may eventually become cultural practices and beliefs in their own right, requiring their own norms, attitudes, and skills. These strategies might be incompatible with what is required for school success, and, thus, caste-like minorities may tend to experience the conflict of two opposing cultural frames of reference—one appropriate for the dominant group and one appropriate for minorities.

Caste-like minorities are reluctant to shift between the two frames because they perceive the frame of the dominant group as clearly inappropriate for them. Since schooling tends to be bound up with the ideals and practices of the majority group, it also tends to be seen as something that is less than appropriate for members of the minority group. Members of the minority community who try to behave like members of the majority community (i.e., learning English, striving for academic success and school credentials) may be ostracized by their peers. The dilemma for such minority students is that they must choose between two competing cultural frames: one that promotes school success and one that does not, but is considered appropriate for a good member of the minority group (Ogbu & Matute-Bianchi 1986; Ogbu 1992; Trueba 1984).

Schweers & Velez (1992) vividly illustrate these points as they describe the conflict that Puerto Ricans face when learning English on the island. In 1902, following the Spanish-American War, when Puerto Rico became an unincorporated territory of the United States, English was declared an offical language of equal status to Spanish. Shortly thereafter, English was imposed on the public school system, not only as a required subject, but also as the preferred language of instruction. Although the policy has changed dramatically since then (in 1992, Spanish was declared the sole official language of government on the island), English still enjoys great prestige among Puerto Ricans, who have held U.S. citizenship since 1917. English represents real political power, the language of the most powerful and influential country in the world, and to most Puerto Ricans is the *sine qua non* for professional advancement and economic security. Schweers and Velez (1992) point out, however, that there has been persistent resistance to the spread and use of English on the island of Puerto Rico throughout the course of this century, citing a 1992 poll that showed that although 83% of respondents favored official status for both English and Spanish on the island, only 20% of the population was reported to be functionally bilingual. As Schweers and Velez (1992, 14) explain, "Many Puerto Ricans resist learning English precisely because of the beliefs and advantages that support its presence on the island."

While the relationship between culture and schooling is one that is extremely complex, one fact again becomes starkly apparent: Although learning English is essential for success in school for all linguistic minority students, the acquisition of English alone in no way guarantees that every linguistic minority student will succeed academically. The question of school achievement is not solely a linguistic one; the cultural messages received by children from both the school and the larger society may influence their feelings about school as well as their feelings about themselves in relation to school. The way in which children view themselves is connected to the way schools (and the larger community) view them.

Chapter 5

Placement Myths

Placement Myth #1: L2 students just need to be placed in an English-speaking environment and they'll learn the language. That's how my grandparents learned English.

Reality: Nonnative English-speaking students must be offered an appropriate education that takes into consideration their developing language. Just being immersed in English in school will not guarantee academic and linguistic success. This is particularly true for older learners, for whom control over complex language is a prerequisite for successful academic learning.

Background/Overview

Although it is true that previously some immigrants to the United States encountered economic success without the benefits of specialized school programs, their success was not dependent on having high levels of proficiency in both spoken and written English. Today's world is considerably different from then. Whereas our immigrant grandparents generally needed no more than oral, interpersonal communication skills in English, at most, in order to succeed in the United States, today's immigrants must reach high levels of literacy in English in order to participate beyond the poverty level. Consequently, simply placing newcomers in an English-speaking environment will not adequately prepare them to participate fully in the life of the nation. Specialized, appropriate educational programs are required by law to ensure that the language and academic needs of L2 students are met (Figure 5–1).

The right to a quality education for language minority students is expressed strongly in a Supreme Court decision known as *Lau v. Nichols* (1974). The court ruled that schools have an obligation to take action to rectify language barriers that result in the exclusion of linguistic minority children from meaningful participation in educational programs (First & Carrera 1988). The suit, which was brought on behalf of Chinese students in the San Francisco Public Schools who spoke little or no English, alleged that approximately half of the Chinese-speaking students needing special instruction were not receiving it, thus creating an unequal educational opportunity for the students. In a unanimous decision, the Supreme Court ruled in favor of the students, stating:

Basic English skills are at the very core of what these public schools teach. Imposition of a requirement that, before a child can effectively participate in the educational program, he must already have acquired those basic skills is to make a mockery of public education. We know that those who do not understand English are certain to find their classrooms wholly incomprehensible and in no way meaningful.

There is no equality of treatment merely by providing students with the same facilities, textbooks, teachers, and curriculum, for students who do not understand English are effectively foreclosed from any meaningful education.

Later in 1974, the Equal Educational Opportunities Act (EEOA) was passed. This act stated that "the failure by an educational agency to take appropriate action to overcome language barriers that impede equal participation by the students in its instructional program" was an unlawful practice that gave individuals a right to sue under the Act. *Appropriate action* was not defined by Congress. However, in 1981, this term was interpreted by judges in the 5th Circuit Court of Appeals in the *Castañeda v. Pickard* decision.

In *Castañeda,* the court outlined a framework with which to review the degree to which equal educational opportunities are provided to language minority students. The framework is a tripartite test that includes the following:

1. A program designed to serve language minority students must be based on educational theory recognized as sound by some experts in the field.

2. It must be implemented effectively, with adequate resources and personnel.

3. After a trial period, it must be evaluated as effective in overcoming language barriers.

By using this test, the court was able to examine the degree to which actions taken by a school district might be deemed "appropriate." The Castañeda decision imposed two other requirements, a dual obligation to (1) teach students English while taking appropriate action to ensure that English language deficiencies do not constitute a barrier to the acquisition of substantive knowledge, and (2) overcome all barriers to an equal education.

This tripartite test established in Castañeda was applied in *Keyes v. School District No. 1 of Denver, Colorado* (1983). The defendant school district asserted its good faith effort to provide services to students in need. The court ruled that good faith alone is not an adequate defense, and stated, "What is required is an effort which will be reasonably effective in producing the intended result of removing language barriers to participation in the instruction programs offered by the district," (576 F. Supp. at 1520). The court also defined additional features of required programs, including the proper identification and classification of students in need of services, at the outset of a student's educational program and at regular intervals throughout, to ensure that progress is being made. (See Figure 5–1 for an overview of legal decisions relevant to the education of language minority students.)

In our work with school districts, we have found that classroom teachers generally feel at a loss when L2 students are placed in their classes, even those teachers who have taken some credential courses or workshops specially designed to prepare them to teach children who come to school speaking a language other than English.

Figure 5–1
Overview of Legal Decisions Relevant to the Education
of Language Minority Students*

SUPREME COURT

1974   *Lau v. Nichols*

Suit by Chinese parents in San Francisco leads to ruling that *identical* education does not constitute *equal* education under Title VI of the Civil Rights Act of 1964. School districts must take affirmative steps to overcome educational barriers faced by non-English speakers. Established that the Office for Civil Rights, under the former Department of Health, Education, and Welfare, has the authority to establish regulations for Title VI enforcement.

1982   *Plyler v. Doe*

Under the Fourteenth Amendment of the U.S. Constitution, the state does not have the right to deny a free public education to undocumented immigrant children.

FEDERAL COURTS

1974   *Serna v. Portales*

The 10th Circuit Court of Appeals found that Spanish-surnamed students' achievement levels were below those of their Anglo counterparts. Ordered Portales Municipal Schools to implement a bilingual/bicultural curriculum, revise procedures for assessing achievement, and hire bilingual school personnel.

1978   *Cintron v. Brentwood*

The Federal District Court for the Eastern District of New York rejected the Brentwood School District's proposed bilingual program on the grounds that it would violate "Lau Guidelines" by unnecessarily segregating Spanish-speaking students from their English-speaking peers in music and art. The court also objected to the program's failure to provide for exiting students whose English language proficiency was sufficient for them to understand mainstream English instruction.

1978   *Ríos v. Reed*

The Federal District Court for the Eastern District of New York found that the Pastchogue-Medford School District's transitional bilingual program was basically a course in English and that students were denied an equal educational opportunity by not receiving academic instruction in Spanish. The court wrote: "A denial of educational opportunities to a child in the first years of schooling is not justified by demonstrating that the educational program employed will teach the child English sooner than a program comprised of more extensive Spanish instruction."

(continued)

1981   *Castañeda v. Pickard*

Reputed to be the most significant court decision affecting language minority students after *Lau*. In responding to the plaintiffs' claim that Raymondville, Texas Independent School District's language remediation programs violated the Equal Educational Opportunities Act (EEOA) of 1974, the 5th Circuit Court of Appeals formulated a set of basic standards to determine school district compliance with EEOA. The "Castañeda test" includes the following criteria: (1) *Theory:* The school must pursue a program based on an educational theory recognized as sound or, at least, as a legitimate experimental strategy; (2) *Practice:* The school must actually implement the program with instructional practices, resources, and personnel necessary to transfer theory to reality; (3) *Results:* The school must not persist in a program that fails to produce results.

1983   *Keyes v. School District No. 1*

A U.S. District Court found that a Denver public school district had failed to adequately implement a plan for language minority students—the second element of the "Castañeda Test."

---

* *Ask NCBE No. 7—What Court Rulings Have Impacted the Education of Language Minority Students in the U.S.?* Reprinted with permission from the National Clearinghouse for Bilingual Education <http://www.ncbe.gwu.edu>

As a consequence, students in mainstream classes are often exposed to a "sink or swim" submersion approach in their schoolday. Students whose teachers are more learner-centered in their approaches, for example, encouraging lots of hands-on experiences and collaborative group work, have more opportunities to understand English and develop their fluency. However, even in these classes, very little instructional time is devoted to their particular needs—teachers frequently say that they have no idea what to expect of their L2 students, and they are hard-pressed to describe in detail what these students are capable of doing, what their immediate needs are, and how they can help their students address their needs.

Placement Myth #2: L2 students' academic success is determined primarily by their ability to learn English.

Reality: Although learning English is essential for school success for all language minority students, the acquisition of English alone in no way guarantees that L2 students will succeed academically.

Background/Overview

The question of school achievement is not solely a linguistic one; the cultural messages received by students from both the school and the larger society may influence their feelings about school as well as their feelings about themselves in relation to school. In addition, the way in which students view themselves is connected to the way that schools (and the larger community) view them. All of these factors influence students' school or academic success.

Language learning is a highly social act. Consequently, social factors such as learner attitudes (e.g., towards the target language, target language speakers, and one's native language and home culture), learning style, prior experience, age, and personality influence the rate of acquisition and the degree to which fluency is acquired in conversational English and reading and writing. (See Second Language Acquisition Myths #1, #2, and #3 for a discussion.)

The length of time that L2 learners appear to need in order to master language for academic purposes accounts for some of the confusion experienced by teachers working with L2 learners. Many L2 students puzzle their teachers because they display relatively proficient English language skills in social settings such as the playground and cafeteria, where contextualized language skills are sufficient. However, when these students return to the classroom, it often seems as if they have lost what English they have learned and are somehow hoodwinking their teachers. It is not unusual to hear teachers comment, "I think they know more than they're letting on. I hear them using English on the playground, yet when it's time for social studies, their English suddenly disappears. Are they trying to fool me so they can get out of doing the work?" Probably not. In many cases, students who have achieved modest levels of contextualized English proficiency are "exited" from support programs that are needed to help them continue the process of acquiring decontextualized language skills and concepts that they need in order to cope with higher order academic knowledge, skills, and processes. This disparity between students' linguistic capabilities in social settings and in academic settings often results in a lack of academic success and the falling behind in content classes such as social studies and science.

This type of mismatch between (oral) language competence and academic competence in English is a common occurrence, and is often seen most starkly in school settings. Older, school-age learners, in particular, require more sophisticated language skills to help them maneuver through complex social and challenging academic situations. Academic learning is characterized by considerable context-reduced language use, that is, situations in which there are few meaningful, contextualized clues to help the learner understand and process the information communicated in the nonnative language. (See Second Language Acquisition Myth #2 for additional discussion of this topic.)

For some students, the mismatch between oral and written levels of proficiency is reversed. That is, some students appear more proficient in literacy contexts than in oral contexts (Saville-Troike 1991). When one of us worked in a newcomer high school, she observed that many of the Chinese speaking students would rarely speak English, yet wrote quite fluently. Part of this level of comfort appeared to be related to the fact that the students, whether from Hong Kong, China, or Taiwan, had received instruction in English prior to leaving their homelands, and this instruction had focused heavily on the printed word. In contrast were many Spanish-speaking students who were considerably more comfortable speaking English than they were reading and writing English. In many cases, the schooling of these students from Central America had been interrupted by war, and very few of them had received any instruction in English prior to entering the United States.

As these situations illustrate, previous schooling can influence L2 levels of acquisition. Another factor related to previous schooling that can influence L2 students' academic success in English is the amount of exposure to content in the native language that students have received. Studies show that children who have had formal academic preparation in a given content area in their native language usually make greater progress initially in the second language (Collier 1989; Cummins 1981a, 1981b). It is clear that for such students who lack basic skills in the first language, learning academic English and the content of an academic setting will be much more challenging than for their counterparts who have received adequate schooling and are literate and performing at grade level in their native languages.

Scenario

Silvia Jaramillo entered the teaching profession as a sixth-grade teacher in a low-income, urban neighborhood where most of the students came from Spanish-speaking homes. As a Latina herself, and the first in her family to earn a college degree, she worked hard to help her students succeed academically. She constantly provided them with challenging and engaging learning experiences that enhanced their academic achievement and allowed them to become fully bilingual and biliterate. She took particular pleasure is seeing the young girls blossom into articulate and thoughtful students who enjoyed invigorating discussions about literature, difficult math problems, and rigorous scientific explorations in both English and Spanish. She was confident that her students were well prepared for junior high and would succeed there, and later in high school.

Not many years passed, however, before Ms. Jaramillo understood that her confidence had been misplaced. At district-wide meetings, she would occasionally talk with junior high teachers about former students, and she realized that her memory of these students was radically different from the students being described to her by her colleagues. Students that she remembered as being animated were described as lethargic. Students that she remembered as being academically gifted were failing classes and close to dropping out. It wasn't until Ms. Jaramillo transferred to a neighboring junior high school that she began to understand what was happening.

She quickly saw that, whereas the elementary school had encouraged bilingualism and biliteracy, the junior high school stressed an English-only approach and did not value or respect students' competence in Spanish. When students spoke Spanish in class, non-Spanish-speaking teachers and students chastised them. Latino students would tease their Latino peers who spoke up in class in English; sometimes they were accused of "acting white." It didn't take long for newly arrived students from the elementary school to realize that their home language was a low-status language in this environment.

Ms. Jaramillo also discovered that a vast majority of students from her former elementary school were rarely placed in advanced classes. Most were in basic math classes rather than pre-Algebra, Algebra, or Geometry classes. Very few were in Gifted and Talented Education (GATE) classes. In the faculty room, the prevailing view among teachers was that the Latino students and their families didn't value education and not much could be asked or expected of them academically. Quickly, Latino students withered under these assaults, stopped studying, and no longer showed enthusiasm for learning. Some students joined gangs, which provided a sense of belonging. When Ms. Jaramillo spoke with her former elementary students about their current academic underachievement, they argued that it wasn't worth trying, as no one expected them to do well in school or out of school. Not only that, it wasn't "cool" to be a good student. Silvia Jaramillo did her best to reverse these developments. She established a Latino club/study group, which attracted small, but growing numbers of students. She petitioned for a Spanish for Spanish Speakers class, which the principal eventually endorsed, albeit skeptically. She held meetings for parents, which were well attended. Nevertheless, it was an uphill battle, as she had to battle entrenched indifference and bias on the part of many educators, as well as disengagement on the part of the students themselves.

Placement Myth #3: L2 students need only about one year in which to learn enough English to be able to succeed academically. Therefore, the emphasis should be on transitioning students out of special programs as quickly as possible.

Reality: There is great variability in how quickly L2 students learn English and in the type of proficiency they reach in conversational and literacy situations. However, most L2 students need from 7 to 10 years in order to acquire academic English on a level comparable to their native-speaking peers.

Background/Overview

There is likely to be great variation in the conceptual development of students who may be at the same stage of oral language development in English. Students who have learned concepts in their native language will more easily handle the concepts when they are introduced in English than will students who have not already had exposure to the concepts. Although students who come to U.S. schools with very little formal schooling bring with them a wealth of experiences, they may not have had much exposure to the kinds of experiences and conceptual development that are at the center of school success in this country. Because skills and strategies often transfer from one language to another (Cummins 1979)—for example, the ability to read, write, or compute—students who have not had much schooling or are not literate in their

Figure 5–2
Supporting Under-Achieving Language Minority Students

- Design and offer sections of foreign language classes for native speakers
- Sponsor clubs for language minority students
- Offer meetings for parents conducted in the native language
- Purchase books and other materials in languages other than English

native languages are likely to need more time and specialized support than are those students whose backgrounds have included considerable schooling or literacy development. (See Figure 5–2 for an overview of how to support underachieving language minority students.)

Scenario

The intermediate-grade faculty at School No. 29 is concerned about variations in the linguistic and academic development of their L2 students, who speak over thirty languages and come from over forty countries. In particular, they are concerned about the children from Guatemala, who seem to have a hard time adjusting to life in the United States and are only slowly acquiring English. In contrast are some students from India and Europe, who are doing much better. The faculty members want to know why there are these stark differences and what they can do to help their less successful students. A consultant from a nearby technical assistance center is meeting with the faculty. At one point, the conversation turns to the progress of students from different language backgrounds:

Frank: Many of my Spanish-speaking students aren't really progressing in English. And when I compare them to the kids from India and Russia that are in my class, there's a huge difference in how quickly they learn and what they're able to do. I'm really concerned about them.

Consultant: Tell me more about the students and what you know about them.

Frank: Well, most of my Spanish-speakers are from Guatemala. I'm not sure if they went to school in Guatemala, but most of them had two years in a Spanish-English bilingual school before transferring to our school.

Alfreda: I don't think they had much schooling in Guatemala from what I remember in the reports from the Placement Center. And, you know, now I come to think of it, I'm not even sure that Spanish is their native language.

Susan: You know, you're right. I made that mistake last month. I thought Magda spoke Spanish at home. I just assumed it. And so when I arranged to meet with her mother, I thought I had covered all bases by having Adelaide [an instructional aide] *meet with us all, to translate. It turned out that Magda's mom didn't speak much Spanish. I guess they speak one of the indigenous languages of Guatemala at home. Right, Adelaide?*

Adelaide: *Uh huh. And I don't speak that language, so it was pretty hard. We managed, though. Sort of.*

Consultant: *What about the kids from India and Russia?*

Pat: *You know, I found out the other day, when we were talking about schooling around the world, that all of my Indian and Russian students seem to have been pretty well educated before they came here. And, lots of them had even had some kind of English classes. So, maybe we shouldn't be so surprised that they are doing that much better on the whole than our students from Central America?*

Consultant: *I think you've hit on some important things that affect second language learners. In the case of the Guatemalan students, it sounds like they've not had much schooling, and even the 2 years in the bilingual program may have been more like schooling in a nonnative language if they didn't speak Spanish. So, if they've not had many school experiences, it's inevitable that they are going to struggle more in learning both English and the content material than are students who have had a lot of schooling in their native language. And came to the United States already somewhat familiar with English.*

Placement Myth #4: Until students learn English, there's no point in trying to teach them content-area subjects.

Reality: It is not necessary (or desirable) to wait until students are fluent in English before teaching them subject matter content. In fact, one effective way of learning a nonnative language is to study content area subject matter through the medium of the nonnative language.

Background/Overview

In the past, schools tended to focus exclusively on the English language development of L2 students. It is clear, however, that it is both possible and desirable to teach L2 students content-area subject matter while they are acquiring English. In fact, it is now believed that one of the best ways of learning a language is to be taught content material in the target language. In recent years, school districts have begun placing newcomers to English in specially designed content-area classes for L2 learners, referred to as either Sheltered English or Specially Designed Academic Instruction in English (SDAIE).

Of course, it is not enough to simply place L2 students in content-area classes intended for native English speakers. Instead, these classes need to be specially designed and taught by teachers who are knowledgeable about both second language acquisition and the content area under study. In particular, the linguistic input needs to be tailored so as to be comprehensible to L2 learners. Most typically, teachers in these classes rely heavily on realia (objects, artifacts, maps, charts, drawings) and gestures, and relate the content to familiar material and experiences, whenever possible.

It is neither desirable nor necessary to decontextualize English language instruction from content instruction and focus instruction on the traditional content of foreign language classes (e.g., verb conjugations, vocabulary drills, and pronunciation exercises). Even in the case of newcomers to an English-speaking environment, English language development that is integrated with developing knowledge about, for example, American school life and procedures, is usually a more effective way of proceeding than simply focusing on English language.

Scenario

In a fourth-grade English Language Development (ELD) class, the students have just begun a unit of study about westward movement, the same social studies content that their native-speaking peers will study that year. The ELD teacher, Mr. Chan, introduced the topic by asking students to interview family members about their own travels and immigration histories. Mr. Chan is a second-generation immigrant himself, and when introducing the topic, he shared his own family history, relying heavily on photographs, drama, drawings, poetry and songs. Students had one week in which to find out as much as they could about their own families' immigrant experiences. They collaborated in compiling a list of questions to ask (e.g., Why did you come to the United States? Which countries did you pass through when coming to the United States? How long did it take to come to the United States? What was the best thing about this trip? What was the worst thing about this trip?). Students knew that they could interview their family members in their native languages. Mr. Chan showed the class how to use simple drawings and captions as notes, which they used when reporting on their families' experiences. He also encouraged them to bring artifacts to share, just as he had done.

When students had completed their family research, they made brief presentations to the class and responded to questions. At the end of each talk, Mr. Chan and the class recorded the data generated on a chart (e.g., country of origin, reason for coming to the United States, countries visited, length of journey, best thing about the trip). In addition, students each had an 18-inch square on the bulletin board on which to post photographs, drawings, artifacts, and information about their families' immigrant experiences.

After this introduction to the movement of people in search of a new life, Mr. Chan asked the class what they knew about westward movement in the United States in the 1800s. Students responded in writing and drawings first (which Mr. Chan used to assess student knowledge of the topic) and then shared their knowledge in a whole-class discussion. Most knew very little, though some of the students had seen cowboy and Indian films and talked about the wars and John Wayne. Over several days, Mr. Chan introduced the class to the topic by reading picture books, using maps to trace pioneer trails and key events, and showing films, videos, and CDs about this era in U.S. history. At the end of each class, the class debriefed by adding data to the chart that they had begun when sharing their family histories. They also added other categories to their chart, including "impact of newcomers on where they settled."

After immersing students in the era, Mr. Chan asked the class to work in groups to generate questions that they now had about westward movement in the United States. The groups' questions ranged from "Why did soldiers kill Indians?" to "How did people stay in touch with their families?" New groups then formed to find answers to these questions. They were given 2 weeks in which to prepare brief presentations for the rest of the class. Mr. Chan steered students to resources that would help them find answers to their questions. At the end of the 2 weeks, the groups made their presentations, which included posters, skits, murals, and poetry. As a final activity in this unit, and as a way to assess how much students had learned, Mr. Chan asked students to reflect, in writing, on what they had learned about westward movement and list any lingering questions. Most students used both words and labeled drawings to record this knowledge. Students then met in small groups to debrief what they had learned. As a whole class, they discussed their lingering questions.

Placement Myth #5: L2 students should be placed in programs for students with handicapping conditions.

Reality: Being a nonnative English speaker is not a handicapping condition or a learning disability, and placing L2 students in special education classes is not usually the appropriate placement for them, unless they have a handicapping condition. (See Assessment Myth #6 for a discussion on assessing L2 students for handicapping conditions.)

Background/Overview

In some states, in the past, being limited in English proficiency was enough to classify students as being in need of special education. In fact, one of us taught ESOL students in Illinois from 1970–1973, and was required to obtain certification as a special education teacher of the "socially maladjusted." Newly arrived immigrant children were quickly placed in special education programs after having been tested in only English, and were labeled mentally retarded, mentally handicapped, or emotionally disturbed. With the passage of Public Law 94-142 (Amendments of Part B of the Education of the Handicapped Act) in 1975, states and school districts were charged with the responsibility of assessing students in their native language (Fradd & Wilen 1990).

Stepped-up activity on the part of the Office of Civil Rights (OCR) in the U.S. Department of Education began in 1991, when districts were told that they could expect closer scrutiny of programs serving language minority students. The OCR said that it would examine three issues in particular: (1) LEP students who were placed in special education programs merely because of their lack of language skills in English, (2) disabled LEP students excluded from special education programs because of their LEP status, and (3) disabled LEP students enrolled in special education programs, but excluded from bilingual programs (Stewart 1993).

Two extremes sometimes prevail with regard to the placement of L2 learners in special education classes. In the past, and even today in some schools, L2 students who do not become fluent in English in a year or so are assessed in English and, based on the test scores, assumed to have a handicapping condition, despite the fact that the assessment was not conducted in the students' dominant language. Consequently, a disproportionate number of L2 students are classified as having a handicapping condition. In contrast are the students who do not make progress over several years in either English or the content areas, and their teachers are reluctant to refer them for assessment for a handicapping condition, thinking that their lack of fluency and academic progress is related only to their L2 status. In both scenarios, L2 students do not receive the most appropriate education and suffer for it.

In some districts, speech and language teachers are used to teach L2 students. This may seem like the best placement for L2 students, given these teachers' background in and knowledge of language development. However, if the speech and language teachers are not fully cognizant of L2 acquisition, it is unlikely that they will be able to provide L2 students with an appropriate education. It should be remembered that there is a huge difference between the developmental delay in language acquisition manifested by children who have language disabilities in their native language and the experience of newcomers to English who already have mastery over their native language and are learning English as a nonnative language.

Scenario

Most of the students in this fourth-grade class are nonnative speakers. A student teacher has just finished reading aloud to the class and has dismissed students to work at learning centers (e.g., a listening center, an independent reading center, a dialogue journal writing center). The classroom teacher is meeting with the journal group, moving from student to student, listening to what they read aloud and then responding in writing to their comments. One of the girls in this group, Pati, spends at least ten minutes writing and erasing letters and at the end of the session, when the bell rings to indicate that students are to pack up, there are only erased letters on her page. As she crosses the classroom to place her journal in her box, she passes the student teacher's university supervisor, who asks Pati if she would show her the journal. Pati shrugs her shoulders and shows it to the visitor. On each page there is a date, and in some cases a word or two also, though the visitor cannot understand the message. Pati and the visitor look at the entry together and the visitor asks her to tell her about the picture. Pati shrugs, so the visitor asks her in Spanish, thinking that perhaps she is more dominant in that language. Pati says that she doesn't know how to write. The visitor asks her what she had wanted to write and she says, "Me fui a Puerto Rico" (I went to Puerto Rico), so the visitor asks her what sounds she hears in "Me." She says "muh," so the visitor suggests that she write that down. Pati looks questioningly and eventually writes a "P." The visitor asks if she can hear any other sounds in "Me" and she says that she doesn't. They continue like this for a couple of minutes. At the end, Pati has written a message that is hard to comprehend.

The visitor wonders if Pati has special learning needs, so when she talks with the student teacher and classroom teacher at recess, she asks about Pati. It turns out that the classroom teacher has had concerns, but because it takes so long in her district to arrange for assessing students, she hasn't bothered to follow up. Pati has been in the district since kindergarten. It turns out that her teachers in previous grades have all had concerns about Pati's lack of progress, but up to that point she has never been tested for special needs. The lack of follow-up appears to have been caused by both lethargy on the part of teachers and the misguided belief that her problems are grounded in her nonnative English-speaking status, even though all of her schooling over the past 4 to 5 years has been in English. Eventually, Pati is assessed by a Spanish-speaking psychologist and is classified as having special learning needs.

Placement Myth #6: When teaching newcomers, it is best to hold off on reading and writing instruction until they have a pretty good grasp of oral English.

Reality: L2 learners should be exposed to meaningful experiences with print in English from early on in their English learning.

Background/Overview

In many schools, students who appear to be orally fluent in English are considered proficient in English. There are two potential problems with this view. First, oral fluency in an interpersonal situation such as the playground may not reflect oral fluency in other, perhaps more challenging situations (Cummins 1981b). For example, carrying on a lunchtime conversation is generally less challenging than defending one's position in an academic debate. Second, oral fluency is not sufficient for school success in this country. Students also need to be proficient readers and writers. It is therefore wise to ensure that all language modes are addressed, and that they are addressed in a variety of contexts (e.g., personal and academic writing, fiction and nonfiction reading, listening to a lecture, and listening to a friend retell a familiar incident).

L2 students, particularly those who have already been schooled in their native language, can draw upon prior knowledge. But, even students who have not been highly educated in their native language can benefit from meaningful reading and writing experiences in English. Urzúa (1987) has documented how nonnative English-speaking Southeast Asian students in the elementary grades can write effectively (and often evocatively) in their nonnative language, albeit with the kinds of errors that one frequently encounters in L2 writing. Students are often fully aware of the needs of their audience when writing, such that children who are in bilingual programs will alter the language of their writing to accommodate the needs of their different audiences (Hudelson & Sema 1993).

Simply exposing L2 students to meaningful print experiences is not, however, enough. Students also need to be taught learning strategies that can enhance their learning of both content and language. More experienced and successful students are distinguished from less experienced and successful learners in the way and degree to which they use carefully chosen learning strategies (e.g., organizing, planning learning, transferring information, and taking notes). It is vital that LEP students be provided with opportunities to become increasingly more aware and critical of their own learning and thinking processes in order that they may have additional learning tools at their disposal (Chamot, Dale, O'Malley & Spano 1992; Chamot & O'Malley 1985; Oxford 1992, 1993).

Scenario

In Mrs. Monson's pull-out ESOL class, third- and fourth-grade recent immigrants sit around a kidney-shaped table. They are tossing around a tissue box covered with a fabric remnant—picture cards of vegetables are attached to the box with rubber bands, and when students catch the box, they have to generate a sentence including the word pictured on the card that is uppermost (e.g., "This is a carrot"). At first, the students are engaged by this activity, but quickly tire of the task. Mrs. Monson alters the activities every few minutes. They embark on several oral and aural language drills and games, and finish the session with jazz chants and songs. Mrs. Monson explains that it would be too hard for the students if she were to ask them to read and write; this is why she focuses exclusively on listening and speaking activities.

In a neighboring school, a similar group of L2 students is meeting with their ESOL teacher, Ms. Andrews. They are sitting in pairs, reading small books written by other ESOL students. They are animated as they read the books, which are stored in a plastic basket on the circular table around which they are sitting. As the students delve into the basket and pick books to read, they laugh at details in the pictures, work together to figure out unfamiliar words, occasionally turn to Ms. Andrews for help, and chat about the content of the book (e.g., "Look her dog," "This mother?"). At the end of about 15 minutes, Ms. Andrews asks the students to finish up their reading so that they can meet together. She explains that everyone has been enjoying the books written by other students, and Joseph and Vladimir have said that they'd like to write their own books. She suggests that everyone might enjoy doing that; the group is enthusiastic. They then brainstorm some possible topics, which Ms. Andrews writes down on chart paper (e.g., "My baby brother," "My family," "Coming to America," "I lost my dog"). She draws simple pictures next to each topic listed so that the students will be able to more readily use the chart as a resource when writing their books. In contrast with Mrs. Monson, Ms. Andrews has found that meaningful literacy experiences support the development of all language modalities; she does not delay introducing her students to reading and writing in English until they are more fluent orally.

Placement Myth #7: English language learners who speak very little English should be placed with younger students so they can more easily learn English.

Reality: L2 students should be placed with their age group because language learning is a socially constructed endeavor.

Background/Overview

Acquiring a nonnative language can be a very stressful experience, and schools should do all they can to reduce the stress. When students are placed with much younger learners, they are invariably isolated from their own age group, which can be extremely stressful and lead to loss of self-esteem. In a discussion of ways to enhance the integration of refugee and immigrant children in schools, Coelho (1994) points out that placing learners with younger students will not cause them to acquire English more quickly than when placed age-appropriately.

For many L2 learners, linguistic and academic success is tied to their social integration. School experiences, in the classroom, in the lunchroom, and in the playground, have the potential to provide L2 learners with multiple language and academic learning opportunities. The types of interactions that learners experience, with their teachers and with their classmates, influence language and academic acquisition. Second language researchers have hypothesized that affective factors such as motivation, self-confidence, and anxiety can have a profound impact on the rate of language acquisition (Dulay and Burt 1977; Krashen 1981). If one accepts this hypothesis, then it follows that being placed in an uncomfortable environment, such as with much younger students, can cause anxiety, which can adversely affect learning.

Although L2 students may come to school with little exposure to or command of English, or with limited formal schooling, they do come to school with rich and varied experiences; the older the students, the greater the likelihood that their life experiences are more complex and varied than those of much younger students. Also, although L2 learners may not speak or be fluent in English, their cognitive processing is likely to be much more developed than that of much younger native English-speaking children.

It should also be remembered that the types of learning experiences that teachers offer their students are geared to the developmental needs of a particular age group. For example, many teachers incorporate a developmental approach to writing instruction, such as one finds in a writers' workshop (Samway 1993b). In a writers' workshop, students generate their own topics, confer with adults and peers on their writing, and are taught writing skills and strategies according to their individual or group needs. Although these basic elements are usually present in any writers' workshop, they frequently look different in different grade levels. For example, in a kindergarten classroom, one is likely to observe considerable variation in how native English-speaking children write (e.g., using scribbles, random letters, or initial sounds to label pictures or write simple narratives). In contrast, in a third-grade classroom, one is unlikely to see students using scribbles or random letters, and texts are frequently longer and more complex. The writing of older beginning speakers of English who have limited knowledge of English is much closer to third graders' writing than it is to kindergartners' writing, as they draw upon their background knowledge of print and attempt to convey fairly complex ideas for which they do not yet have the language. For example, Taylor (1990) found that her intermediate-grade newcomer ESL students cleverly used symbols to express concepts for which they did not yet have complete command in English (e.g., using a "X" to indicate a negative).

Even L2 students from a nonalphabetic language (e.g., Chinese or Arabic) will not need the same kind of exposure to, discussions about, and instruction in the English alphabet and spelling that 5-year-old native speakers of English need.

Research on the effects of group work and cooperative learning on academic achievement further underscores the importance of being placed with one's peers. Group work is thought to be beneficial to L2 learners by increasing the amount of practice and quality of practice in English than would otherwise be available (Long & Porter 1985). Group work and cooperative learning also help to provide more comprehensible input and output, create a positive affective climate, and increase student motivation. In other words, meaningful interactions with peers build on the way in which language and knowledge are socially constructed, and provide L2 learners with enhanced opportunities for both linguistic and academic input and output (Kagan 1986; Slavin 1990).

Scenario

It is Thursday morning on a cool October morning and the school secretary at Hillside Elementary School knocks on the door of the principal and pushes it open. "We've got another one," she announces, almost in a whisper. "She wouldn't say anything to me, but I think she speaks Spanish. Her dad says her name's Graci something. He doesn't speak much English." The principal sighs, stands up, and moves into the general meeting area of the office, where she extends her hand in greeting to the man who is standing by the door. "Hello," she says, "I'm Ms. Gray, the principal." Graciela's father says, "Little English," and gestures to emphasize that he does not speak much English. He puts his arm around the wide-eyed, silent girl who stands close by him. "This Graciela. She 9," he says. After spending twenty minutes trying to communicate, Ms. Gray takes Graciela (who hasn't spoken a word since entering the office) and her father to a first-grade classroom. She has decided to place Graciela two grades below her age group because she doesn't speak English and is small for her age. In this way, she hopes that the girl will fit in more easily and learn English more quickly . . . and be less of a struggle for the teachers.

In fact, Graciela takes several months before she is comfortable using English extensively, and during that time she becomes increasingly more withdrawn. She does not play with the other first graders, rarely talks with them, and during recesses she wanders over to the playground where third and fourth graders play with balls and jump ropes. One day she indicates in a dialogue journal that she is sad to be with such young children. She does this through a picture and a few words (a picture of a girl who is crying that is labeled "graciela big sad" and to one side a group of smaller children labeled "kids lidel"). After reading Graciela's journal entry, her teacher talks with her and realizes that Graciela is very unhappy at being with much younger children. The teacher concludes that Graciela should have been placed with her own age group because she is much more mature than the first graders and being with them doesn't appear to be enhancing her language or academic abilities. Although some of the activities that the class takes part in engage Graciela (e.g., the dialogue journal writing, which allows her to talk with her teacher in a one-on-one setting on a regular basis, and some of the shared reading, in which the whole class shares the reading of an enlarged version of a predictable story, poem or song), many of the other activities do not appear to engage or challenge either her linguistic or cognitive needs (e.g., single-digit addition worksheets).

Graciela's teacher is right. She should have been placed in a third-grade class so that she could benefit from the amount of learning that comes from being with one's peers. Language learning is a socially constructed process. Although it is likely that Graciela would have gone through an extended silent period, even in a third-grade class, she would have been able to benefit from interactions with her peers, and her cognitive development would have been stretched by these age- and developmentally appropriate learning experiences (Wong Fillmore 1976).

Placement Myth #8: L2 students can't be expected to achieve to the same level as fluent English-speaking students, and teachers need to lower their expectations for L2 students.

Reality: Although L2 learners may not be able to produce native-like English, teachers must guard against lowering expectations.

Background/Overview

Teacher expectations can have a profound impact on student achievement. Many studies of teacher perceptions and expectations can be found in the literature on school achievement (e.g., Brophy & Good 1974; Carew & Lightfoot 1979; Rist 1970; Rosenthal & Jacobson 1968). While these studies are not concerned specifically with L2 students, they suggest that teacher perceptions and expectations play a significant role in the education of all students. Although the effects of these perceptions and expectations are not clear, it seems likely that inaccurate perceptions on the part of teachers make it that much harder to plan appropriate instruction that meets L2 students' needs. The effects of teacher expectations also have been explored in more consumer-oriented media, such as the movie, *Stand and Deliver*, the true story of Jaime Escalante, a high school math teacher, who battled with his peers to teach calculus at his inner-city high school; he succeeded in offering the course, and his students, of whom little had been expected in the past, were outstanding students.

One of the most subtle forms of bias manifests itself in low expectations for students based on their membership in certain racial (e.g., African American), ethnic (e.g., Latino or Tongan), or socioeconomic (e.g., low-income or working-class) groups. Low expectations are reflected in the kinds of classes that are offered to some English language learners in junior and senior high schools (Minicucci & Olsen 1992). Low expectations are reflected in the kinds of learning events that students of all ages are asked to engage in, for example, an emphasis on recall of information tasks versus higher order thinking (Schinke-Llano 1983). Low expectations are also reflected in how well the faculty and staff know and understand the communities from which the students come and the kinds of comments that they make about the students (e.g., saying, "These parents don't care if their children get an education or not. If they did, they'd come to open house and conferences," without knowing that many low-income, nonnative English-speaking parents feel acutely uncomfortable in the English-dominant school environment.).

How teachers use language with students appears to be influenced by teachers' perceptions of students' linguistic abilities. These perceptions, in turn, may affect not only the quantity and quality of cognitively challenging language a teacher provides to L2 students, but also students' access to learning. For example, Schinke-Llano (1983) observed twelve monolingual English-speaking teachers working with fifth and sixth graders. All had classes made up of native English speakers and L2 learners. Her research revealed that the teachers interacted less frequently with the L2 learners than with their native English-speaking counterparts. She also found that when interactions did occur with L2 students, they were significantly different in type: The interactions with L2 students tended to be managerial in nature, rather than instructional. Finally, she found that even when the same type of interaction occurred with both groups of students, the teachers' interactions were briefer with L2 students than with the English-speaking students.

Although Schinke-Llano offered several explanations for these instances of what is often described as "foreigner talk" (that is, adjusting the structure and use of one's language so that it may be understood by those who are perceived by the speaker as incapable of functioning adequately in the language), she offered two that are particularly noteworthy. First, she speculated that the pattern of interactions may have been due to the seating arrangements in the classrooms she observed. In over half of the classrooms, L2 students were seated in the rear of the room. Schinke-Llano further suggested that there may have been a relationship between the students' seating position and the teachers' perceptions of the L2 students' ability to participate in the class. That is, those students who were perceived by teachers as most able to participate were generally placed closer to the instructional heart of the classroom, near the teacher.

The second and most compelling explanation offered by Schinke-Llano was that the teachers avoided interacting with the students for fear of embarrassing them. Implied in this explanation, however, is that teachers assumed that the students would be unable to answer or do well—and their perceptions of the students influenced the way in which they interacted with them.

Schinke-Llano's research leads to two intriguing questions. First, if teachers' perceptions of students' linguistic and cognitive abilities are inaccurate, what are the possible consequences for students? Second, given that teachers' interactions with L2 students appear to be different, can these interactions be monitored and modified so that they facilitate linguistic and cognitive development? Recently, much research and many curriculum development efforts have centered on this second question. The promotion of content-based instruction and whole school environments that foster the achievement of L2 learners appear to show great promise for facilitating such language and cognitive growth. (See also Handscombe 1994; Hudelson 1994; McKeon 1994; Samway 1993a, 1993b.)

In some schools and districts, high goals are set for certain groups of students (e.g., students from China, Vietnam, and Russia), whereas much lower goals are set for other groups of students (e.g., Southeast Asian students whose schooling has been interrupted by war, or students from Mexico). Although prior schooling and academic achievement are important issues to consider when establishing individual goals for students, lowering one's expectations based on group membership is discriminatory, dangerous, and harmful to learners.

Scenario

At the Northern California Institute on Latino Newcomer Students (1991), a conference devoted to exploring the education of Latino high school students, a panel of students described their school experiences in the United States. Seventeen-year-old Carlos told of how he came from Peru a year earlier. Despite the information that his Peruvian school had sent about the classes he had taken, many of which would be considered advanced placement in U.S. schools (e.g., trigonometry and chemistry), he was put in general math and science classes. Another student, Francisca, the daughter of farmworkers, aspired to go to college, but she had been placed in only two classes one year, ESOL and PE, and spent the rest of the year either working in the school office or in study halls. It was not hard to understand their anguish and frustration at being misplaced (or unplaced in classes, as Francisca was). The overriding message that these eloquent young people shared was, "Get to know us and challenge us."

Chapter 6

Assessment Myths

Assessment Myth #1: The only assessments that we need to do with L2 learners are those that determine whether they are LEP.

Reality: Assessment should serve several purposes, including assessing students' performance and determining program effectiveness.

Background/Overview

Assessment for all students is an area that is receiving increased scrutiny. For L2 students, assessment needs to be unbiased and equitable. Assessment has many functions and outcomes, including placement of students, diagnosis of students' progress and needs, and program accountability. See Figure 6–1 for an overview of assessment functions.

Assessment for Placement Decisions

The first assessment tasks in which schools engage when L2 newcomers enter a district are to determine whether they are LEP and where they should be placed (e.g., which grade, which program, which teacher). In many districts, this is done in a cursory fashion, to comply with legal requirements and qualify for funding. However, it can and should be done so as to ensure that L2 students are placed appropriately and that teachers have sufficient information to be able to plan an effective initial program. In many districts, initial assessment is not conducted by classroom teachers (bilingual or regular education). Instead, it is conducted by a variety of personnel, including ESOL teachers, instructional aides, and central office employees. These people usually score and interpret the data, and make placement recommendations. Subsequently, teachers with primary responsibility for teaching L2 learners generally receive some basic, often rudimentary background information on students (e.g., native language, language spoken at home, dominant language, previous schooling), along with a classification of language minority status: non-English proficient (NEP), LEP, or fluent English proficient (FEP). These labels can be helpful in understanding the degree to which students are familiar with or fluent in English (at least

47

Figure 6–1
Why Assess L2 Learners?

- Placing students appropriately
- Diagnosing students' progress and needs
- Assessing students' performance
- Determining program effectiveness

in the test-taking situation), but they should be viewed with caution because they do not usually provide detailed information on a variety of issues that are critical for teachers, including students' linguistic and academic performance in English and the native language (oral language development and literacy); learning strategies, strengths, and needs; or past educational experiences. After placement, teachers can use ongoing formal and informal diagnostic assessments to modify instructional plans, if necessary.

Assessment for Diagnostic Purposes

When assessing L2 students, the procedures used should fulfill clear purposes, for example, to determine the kinds of miscues students make when orally describing an event, reading an unfamiliar text, or writing an information piece. These assessments should generate information that can assist teachers' instructional planning and help students become linguistically and academically more successful. Whenever possible, these assessments should also reveal what students are able to do in the L1 and L2, both linguistically and academically, as there is frequently a mismatch between what children can accomplish in their native language and in the new language, English (Ammon 1985). For example, students may understand the process of photosynthesis in their native language due to prior schooling, but because of their lack of familiarity with English vocabulary, they may give the impression that they do not understand anything about photosynthesis. This type of information is of use to teachers, as it is usually much easier (and a very different instructional objective) to teach the vocabulary of photosynthesis in English to L2 students who already know about the concept than it is to teach the concept through the L2 (English) to students for whom it is a new concept.

In the United States, there is a heavy reliance on large-scale, norm-referenced, standardized testing to assess individual students, as well as entire programs. Regrettably, these assessments rarely provide answers to the questions that teachers ponder. For example, the most commonly used language and reading/language arts tests (e.g., Bilingual Syntax Measure [BSM] and California Test of Basic Skills [CTBS]) are grounded in the decontextualized use of language (e.g., reading and writing tests that involve multiple choice and fill-in-the-blank items rather than real reading and writing tasks). These tests do not measure learners' processes and strategies when they listen, speak, read, and write—information that is useful to teachers. Similarly, norm-referenced, standardized tests of academic content often rely heavily on knowledge of language and literacy, which confounds how one might interpret the test results. For example, are L2 students' scores on these tests grounded in their knowledge of English or their knowledge of the content or a combination of both? Norm-referenced, standardized test scores are rarely helpful to teachers, sometimes because the results are not available for many months, but in large measure because the tests do not investigate what they claim to assess. (See Assessment Myth #5 for a discussion of effective diagnostic assessment tools.)

Assessment for Program Accountability

Program evaluation has traditionally been completed in order to comply with funding guidelines (e.g., for Title I or Title VII) or state regulations. Only rarely is it viewed as an ongoing and integral part of a program, providing continuous feedback to administrators, faculty, staff, parents, and students. Many teachers and administrators often complain that the measures that are most commonly used to judge a program's success (usually norm-referenced, standardized tests) do not measure the goals and accomplishments of the program.

In some states, all students are assessed on the same tests, in English, regardless of their fluency in English and ability to understand the test directions and items. This would be equivalent to non-Japanese-speaking Americans being assessed in Japanese—and then their language and literacy skills and academic achievement being established based on these results. Clearly, the outcomes of these testing policies are often predictable (e.g., LEP students don't usually score very high on them) and potentially very harmful to students (e.g., LEP students are tracked into lower ability, less challenging classes based on the test scores).

This situation occurred in California in the 1997–1998 academic schoolyear. The state mandated that all students take the Standardized Testing and Reporting (STAR) exam in English in order to generate baseline data on the achievement of all students in English. Although 20% of the student body in California's schools are LEP (800,000 students), they were not exempted from the test. Because this action paralleled Proposition 227, which bans instruction in the native language of students in California, many educators and advocates for nonnative English-speaking students viewed the action as an attack on language minority students. One district, San Francisco USD, refused to administer the test to LEP students who had not been in ESL or bilingual programs for 3 years, unless teachers felt students were ready or parents requested that their children take the test. Later, two other San Francisco Bay Area districts (Berkeley and Oakland) intervened in the case on behalf of students and sued to suppress the scores of LEP students. But, after a California Superior Court judge in San Francisco lifted the ban on publishing the test scores, the State Department of Education posted scores on the Internet. However, in this July 1998

California Superior Court ruling (*California Dept. of Education v. San Francisco USD* 1998), the judge also asserted that the state cannot force school districts to place the 1998 STAR scores in the permanent records of students who have been in the United States for fewer than 30 months, make academic decisions based on students' scores, or share the scores with parents. In this way, the judge concurred with critics of the test that administering it in English could be damaging to LEP students.

There should be no question about educators and schools being held accountable for providing a challenging and appropriate education that leads to student success. This is in the best interests of all students, particularly LEP students, for whom academic success may be prejudiced by low expectations and inappropriate placement in academic classes. However, large-scale assessments that are considered to be a way to achieve accountability often become highly charged and vested with political overtones, as happened in California with the administration of the STAR test.

The most useful program evaluation plans provide ongoing feedback to the district, program personnel, and parents and community members. Also, a thorough program evaluation is not limited to single-issue assessment. Instead, it considers a variety of issues, including: (1) program vision; (2) student identification and placement procedures; (3) assessment procedures; (4) expectations for students; (5) student achievement; (6) curriculum, learning environments, and instructional practices; (7) recruitment and retention of highly qualified and successful staff (8) staff development; and (9) parent and community involvement. If the evaluation plan is to reflect program goals, it is essential that classroom teachers and other faculty and staff are involved right from the beginning in designing both the program and evaluation plan. Effective program evaluation is continuous and may change in response to what is learned from the ongoing evaluation of the program. (See Figure 6–2 for a summary of assessment purposes.)

Academic Standards

In recent years, in response to calls for the school success of all students, content-area standards have been developed on the local, state, national, and international levels (e.g., National Board for Professional Teaching Standards 1996; National Council of Teachers of English & International Reading Association 1996; Teachers of English to Speakers of Other Languages [TESOL] 1997). All of these standards recognize the rights of L2 learners to have "unrestricted access to grade-appropriate instruction in challenging academic subjects, and ultimately to lead rich and productive lives" (Teachers of English to Speakers of Other Languages 1997, 2–3). That is, L2 students must have opportunities to learn English while also developing content knowledge. TESOL's ESL standards were developed to assist teachers in implementing content standards developed by other professional groups and organizations, and they are designed to address the needs of ESOL students in grades pre-K through 12. In addition to highlighting the prominent role of language in content-area learning, the standards also explore the developmental needs of ESOL students and offer guidance to teachers on how to best meet the needs of their ESOL students. TESOL has also published a framework for assessing students' attainment of the ESL standards (TESOL 1998).

Figure 6–2
What to Consider When Assessing L2 Learners

- Initial assessment (for placement purposes):
  - Native language and languages spoken in the home
  - Dominant language (oral and literacy)
  - Prior schooling/educational experiences
  - Linguistic and academic development in L1
  - English language fluency (aural, oral, and literacy)
- Diagnostic assessment (for instructional purposes):
  - In L1 and L2, whenever possible (oral and literacy)
  - Learning strategies, strengths, and needs
  - Aligned with standards
- Program assessment (for accountability purposes):
  - Provides ongoing feedback to district, program personnel, and community
  - Assessment Plan considers the following:
    - Program vision
    - Student identification and placement procedures
    - Assessment procedures
    - Expectations for students
    - Student achievement
    - Curriculum
    - Learning environments
    - Instructional practices
    - Recruitment and retention of highly qualified staff
    - Staff development
    - Parent and community involvement

Scenario

It is a gloomy February morning, just a few days before the much-anticipated February break, and Margaret Parker, an experienced fifth-grade teacher, peers around the door of her principal's office. When she sees that David Garcia has just finished a telephone conversation, she knocks on the door softly, enters the room, waits a few seconds for him to greet her, and then launches into what has prompted this visit during her prep period:

Margaret: David, you know that I just got two new students this morning? Omar and Angelina? No, it's Omid and Angelina. Well, neither of them speaks English. (David nods and glances over at a pile of papers lying on his desk.) OK, fine, I did what I've done before: I got other kids to take responsibility for them, to show them around the room and talk with them and make them feel welcome. But, you know, I know absolutely nothing about them, and I don't know what I'm going to do with them. At least the other ESL students I've had in the past spoke some English, but these two haven't said anything to me yet. It must be awful for them. It is for me.

David: I know how difficult it must be for you, Margaret. I know how much you care about your students, and you want them to do well. Hang on a minute. (He leans across the desk.) Some information came on those two students and I forgot to send the files along to you this morning when they arrived. Sorry. Let's take a look at them.

David picks up the pile of papers and extracts two manila folders. He passes one of the folders to Margaret, and they spend the next 2 or 3 minutes reading through them. Margaret is the first to speak:

Margaret: Well, at least there's some information here. Apparently, Omid speaks Farsi. Do you think that's anything like Arabic? If it is, maybe I can have Mohammed take him under his wing. I'll check with Mohammed.

David: I'm not sure about the Arabic, but I know that the print for Farsi isn't like English. I think it's got those squiggles and dots over the letters. And don't you read it from right to left? It would be a big help to him, and you, too, if he's already been exposed to some English. If we're in luck, he's not speaking because he's just overwhelmed.

Margaret: (Laughs) Not likely, knowing my luck! And, take a look at this. He's a level 1 on the LAS. Doesn't that mean that he doesn't speak any English?

David: (Nods) What does it say about his prior schooling?

Margaret: (Opens up the folder and picks up the intake form). Alright. It says he went to school in Iran and was an OK student. Which means he's not new to math and reading and all those lovely school things. And, look at this, he studied German. That may help him a bit. You know, I took German in high school. Years ago! (Both laugh) I don't speak it though, but maybe I can unearth enough to make a connection with him. I need to talk with Pat (the ESOL teacher) and make sure she includes him in her schedule.

Margaret and David continue in this way, building up profiles on the two new students from the data gathered in the intake interview conducted by a bilingual district assessor. They find that Angelina is Portuguese-speaking and scored on a level 2 of the LAS, indicating that she has some understanding of and ability to speak English. This is her second school since arriving in the United States four months earlier. Omid is a recently arrived student from Iran. Before Margaret leaves David's office, he checks to see how she's now feeling about her two new ESOL students:

David: I'm sorry about not getting those files to you earlier, Margaret, but this has been very interesting. How are you feeling about Angelina and Omid now?

Margaret: Well, at least I now know something about them. And after I've talked with

Pat, I'm sure I'll feel even better. She's always so helpful, and the kids enjoy working with her.

David: That's great. But, what about the day-to-day teaching that you'll be handling? What will you do now?

Margaret: *(Pause and sighs)* I think I have to remind myself that for a few days they need time to just get used to us and our routines and maybe some of the basic classroom vocabulary. I'm going to ask for volunteers to buddy up with them, maybe three or four each. I'll need to spend some time teaching them how to help their buddies. Maybe I don't, though. I remember Pat mentioning at that faculty meeting last semester that that's something she can do, so I think I'll ask her if she can spend some time with the volunteers from my class. She'd do a much better job of it than I ever could. *(Pause)* I know it would be easy for me to forget about them if other kids are taking care of them, so I need to make sure to spend some time with them each day. Maybe I can do that during SSR, once everyone is settled. That reminds me that I need to check with Gloria (the district's bilingual resource teacher) about books in Farsi and Portuguese or bilingual books, so there are books they can read. I wonder if they have any books at home? They could bring them in for SSR. *(Pause)* I think that when I read aloud for the next couple of weeks, I'll read patterned picture books and poetry and either use those big book versions or put them on the overhead. The kids have been bugging me to spend more time on poetry, so that should work out fine. I was going to do a picture book study anyway because they're going to be writing books for their younger buddies, and they really enjoy reading books like Brown Bear, Brown Bear. Several of them have said that that's the kind of book they're going to write. This should also make it easier for Angelina and Omid. At least it should be more understandable than if I were to read a novel. Maybe I could read some nonfiction, also, as they come with lots of illustrations. *(Pause)* I need to check with Maria (her cross-age teaching partner) to see if she has any Farsi- or Portuguese-speaking students. Wouldn't that be great if she did? I can't remember. *(Pause)* I should be writing all this down so I don't forget.

David: Yeah. It sounds like you're well on your way, though. How about math and science and social studies?

Margaret: That's going to be tough. They've both been in school, so they must have had math and some science and social studies. I need to check up on that. I'll check with the Intake Center to see what they've found out. If they've assessed that, why isn't it here in the folder?

David: I don't know. It should be. Maybe I can call the Intake Center for you?

Margaret: Thanks, that would help a lot. When you talk with them, can you find out what kind of math and science and social studies Angelina and Omid have done in the past? Also, I'm wondering if the Center has bilingual glossaries of content-area terminology that we could give to the kids. Maybe Pat knows of resources like that? I bet my kids would love to make them up, if they don't! We could market them! I'm getting a bit carried away here, aren't I! *(They laugh)* *(Pause)* What I need to do is to observe them several times each day, at different times of the day, *and keep notes on what I see them doing. That, and checking in with them as much as I can, should help me get a sense of what they're able to do in English. We're about to start an inquiry study on local geography, which is coming at a good time, as so much of that will be pretty hands-on. You know, field trips, films, and CDs. And we've got a couple of speakers who are really excellent. They don't just ramble on and on. They bring lots of objects and slides and get the kids involved. Now I come to think of it, bilingual glossaries of terminology for that inquiry study would help, too. Am I asking for too much?*

David: Uh Uh. (Shakes head) You know what you need. It can't harm to ask for it. If you like, while I'm talking with the Intake Center, I'll also check to see what they know of in terms of geography materials in Portuguese and Farsi.

Margaret: Thanks. (She gets up to leave) You know, when I came in here, I was a bit ticked off. (They laugh) Thanks for your ear and help. It feels a whole lot better to know something about these two youngsters and to have an idea of how I can help them.

(See Figure 6–3 for an overview of strategies for welcoming and integrating students.)

Assessment Myth #2: We teach everyone equally in our school, and we don't need to know who is LEP and who isn't.

Reality: Educators need to know as much about students as possible so that students are provided with the best educational experience possible.

Background/Overview

We sometimes visit classrooms in which teachers say, "Students are students, so I don't want to know who is LEP." The underlying sentiment appears to be grounded in a wish not to be the recipients of other people's biases. While we respect the effort by these teachers to treat all students equally, we believe that they are in danger of doing their students a tremendous disservice by not recognizing that all students have specials strengths and needs. Being a nonnative English speaker is one of those special needs. L2 students' prior life and educational experiences are likely to influence their linguistic and academic progress, and to ignore these factors is to deny the backgrounds and needs of L2 students.

We also respect such teachers' concerns that assessment procedures and data often reflect a deficit view of learners (e.g., focusing on what students cannot do rather than on what they are able to do and appear to be about ready to master). Similarly, we have the utmost respect for teachers who are dedicated to continuously assessing their students' strengths, accomplishments, and needs. Nevertheless, we believe that it is not in the best interests of students for their teachers to be uninformed about their L2 status, past experiences, and needs.

Figure 6–3
Welcoming and Integrating ESOL Students into the Regular Education Classroom

- Allow time to become familiar with the class
- Use peer buddies
- Observe students often and in many situations
- Spend time with ESOL students each day
- Locate books and other materials in L1
- Allow ESOL students to use native languages
- Read intake and past schooling information
- Select instructional materials and topics that build on ESOL students' knowledge

Scenario

Mai Nguyen is 12 years old and has just entered seventh grade at a small, urban junior high school, Martin Luther King Junior. When she arrived in the United States from Vietnam 2 years earlier, she was 10 years old and was placed in a regular education fifth-grade class, as the district did not have a Vietnamese-English bilingual program. Her teacher, Miss Harris, was certified to teach LEP students by virtue of passing a multiple-choice state exam. Mai remained with Miss Harris for the 2 years that she spent in the elementary school, in part because Miss Harris was one of the few upper grade teachers who had received her supplementary ESOL teaching certificate, and in part because Miss Harris had a multiage fifth- and sixth-grade class, which meant that she kept half the class from one year to the next. By the end of her sixth-grade year at the elementary school, Mai had not made much progress in English—she was hard to understand, had difficulty expressing herself in writing, struggled in reading, and had not made many friends in the class. Over the course of the 2 years that Mai was her student, Miss Harris never read her cumulative folder. Although she was concerned about Mai's lack of progress, she attributed it to her L2 status and believed that she would catch up in time. She recommended that Mai be placed in the ESOL program at the junior high school.

When Mai entered Martin Luther King Junior High, she was placed in a sheltered English language arts and social studies class with Mr. Abrahams. As was his custom, he read each student's cumulative folder before the beginning of the semester, and saw that when Mai had entered the school district, the bilingual assessor had noted that Mai had suffered from repeated ear infections, which affected her hearing some of the time. Teachers were asked to monitor her hearing and seek additional assessment, if loss of hearing was thought to be a problem.

Figure 6–4
Tests Commonly Used for L2 Census Purposes

TITLE	GRADE LEVELS	LANGUAGES	MODALITIES ASSESSED
Basic Inventory of Natural Language (BINL)	K–12	English and 32 other languages	Assesses (1) oral language dominance and (2) oral language proficiency: fluency (no. of words generated), syntactic complexity, and average sentence length
Bilingual Syntax Measure I (BSM I)	K–2	English and Spanish	Assesses oral language proficiency; focuses on grammatical structures
Bilingual Syntax Measure II (BSM II)	3–12	English and Spanish	
IDEA Proficiency Tests (IPT)	K–adult	English and Spanish	Assesses oral proficiency and reading and writing ability; measures content such as vocabulary, syntax, and reading for understanding
Language Assessment Scales I (LAS I)	1–5	English and Spanish	Assesses oral proficiency and reading and writing ability; measures vocabulary, minimal pairs, listening comprehension, and story retelling
Language Assessment Scales II (LAS II)	6–12	English and Spanish	

Mr. Abrahams decided to observe Mai closely for a week, but it didn't take him long to discover that Mai seemed to have fairly profound hearing loss. He found that when he stood behind Mai and spoke to her, she never responded, but when he faced her, she did. He also noticed that when there were class discussions and students had their backs to each other, as often happens when four to five desks are clustered together, Mai seemed lost in thought, but when students faced each other in a circle, Mai was attentive (possibly because she could lip read, Mr. Abrahams hypothesized). He immediately contacted the Placement Center and by the end of the month, Mai had been assessed by a Vietnamese-speaking speech and language teacher, who found that she had significant hearing loss.

Assessment Myth #3: Intake assessment tools, such as the Bilingual Syntax Measure (BSM) and the Language Assessment Scales (LAS), provide sufficient information for the appropriate placement and teaching of L2 students.

Reality: These assessment tools are designed for a very specific and limited purpose, such as to determine relative language proficiency and fluency in English. They are not all-encompassing assessment tools, so teachers will need to continue to assess students, using appropriate tools and procedures, in order to make informed instructional decisions.

Background/Overview

Some districts have a well-designed and well-implemented intake procedure that ensures that students' language, literacy, and academic background are assessed thoroughly, and that they are subsequently placed in appropriate classes. However, many problems surround the intake–placement process. In many school districts, initial assessment is not conducted by the teachers and the information is rarely shared with them. In some cases, teachers steadfastly refuse to read the records because they prefer to form their own impressions of students. We have noticed, however, that in their efforts to resist what is often a deficit view of students as reported in records (e.g., "Cannot speak any English" versus "Was able to give her name and age when I asked her in English"), an inordinate amount of time may pass before teachers ever get to know their LEP students.

In many cases, state departments of education have compiled approved lists of tests that are used for census purposes (e.g., to identify how many LEP students are in the district). When used for census or program evaluation purposes, students are generally tested upon arrival in the school district and at the end of the schoolyear. The tests listed below are frequently on those lists:

Basic Inventory of Natural Language (BINL)—grades K–12

Bilingual Syntax Measure I (BSM I)—grades K–2

Bilingual Syntax Measure II (BSM II)—grades 3–12

IDEA Oral Language Proficiency Test I (IPT I)—grades K–6

IDEA Oral Language Proficiency Test II (IPT II)—grades 7–12

Language Assessment Scales I (LAS I)—grades 1–5

Language Assessment Scales II (LAS II)—grades 6–12

See Figure 6–4 for an overview of key features of these language tests.

Although widely used, these tests tend to be of little use to classroom teachers, particularly if the teachers have not administered the tests, or test scores and other information are not made immediately available to teachers. Other limitations of these tests include the following: (1) several of the tests (BINL, BSM, IDEA) are primarily measures of oral language and do not provide information on students' literacy development, (2) none of these tests assess students' linguistic and learning strategies and processes, (3) the assessment tool is sometimes improperly administered so that available data are not necessarily accurate, and (4), sometimes the data gathered by the tests are used strictly for record-keeping and funding purposes (e.g., for Title I or Title VII), rather than being shared with teachers.

If these tests are used, they need to be administered rigorously, following the guidelines in the manual. However, to gain a more accurate and complete picture of a student, the assessment should also take into account native language and literacy proficiency, as well as previous schooling, talents, and special interests. Determining such details can often be accomplished with the help of brief interviews in English and the native language. It is also important to talk with caregivers and interpret any records that may have arrived with the student. Data going to teachers should be thoroughly readable and useful. That is, a test score may be of little help to a teacher, whereas the comment that a student is a fluent reader in Urdu, understands simple questions in English (e.g., "What's your name?" or "How old are you?"), is able to respond in single words and gestures, and is particularly interested in astronomy can help a teacher prepare learning experiences for the newcomer. Initial assessment is best conducted by a knowledgeable person.

Scenario

Once a week, twenty-three teachers from several school districts meet in the evening at a local university for a graduate class focusing on the assessment of L2 students. One of the assignments requires them to become very familiar with a state-approved ESL/bilingual test and to investigate how the test is used in local schools. They have to administer the test themselves, interview teachers and other district personnel who have either administered the test or supervised its administration, and read articles relating to the test. Each of the teachers signs up for a test; in some cases, more than one person works with the same instrument and when this happens, they work as a team. Class members also act as resources for each other, providing each other with information from their own districts.

When class members report back on how the tests are administered, it becomes clear that there is considerable confusion in the districts (at least at the level of teachers and those administering the tests) about the purpose of the tests and how they should be administered. Three common findings emerge:

1. *Classroom teachers usually receive the tests results . . . eventually, but rarely find the data helpful.*

2. *The tests provide classroom teachers with labels for their L2 students, such as English level 1, 2, 3, 4, 5 or non-English proficient (NEP), limited English proficient (LEP), and fluent English proficient (FEP). It is rare for teachers to receive additional information, whether about students' past school experiences or about their linguistic and academic strengths, experiences, and needs.*

3. *Test administration directions are rarely followed as directed. In fact, in some cases, the test administrators have never seen the administration manuals. When this happens, results are often very distorted (e.g., when test administrators read the reading section aloud to students or translate listening test items).*

When the class discusses reasons for these violations of testing protocol, the teachers conclude that it is almost always done out of concern for the students, such as not wanting to see them labeled negatively. It is very clear that assessment is most commonly viewed as a means to judge students and label them; in only a few cases is assessment seen as an integral part of learner-centered teaching.

The professor urges the teachers to share their findings with the school districts; groups of teachers from three districts eventually meet with their administrators. In each case, noticeable changes in initial testing procedures follow. In these districts, one or more of the following actions result from the teachers' investigations: (1) Test manuals are provided for all of the L2 assessors, (2) districts stress in meetings and workshops the importance of following the directions exactly as printed, and (3) staff development is offered to all teachers, principals, and instructional aides about the tests, how to interpret the data, and how to supplement the data provided by the tests with other, ongoing assessment procedures.

Assessment Myth #4: Placement centers are an expensive and not very useful alternative to initial assessment in schools.

Reality: Placement centers can often accomplish thorough initial assessments of L2 students and provide ongoing support and resources to instructional staff.

Background/Overview

Particularly in the case of districts that are home to large numbers of L2 students, establishing a placement-assessment center may be the most effective and efficient means of assessing and placing students. In these centers, assessors are usually certified, experienced teachers who are either bilingual or ESOL specialists. Often, they are assisted by native speakers of languages that are not spoken by these specialists; in many cases, these assistants were teachers in their home countries, but have not yet received their U.S. teaching certificate. Placement center specialists frequently fulfill multiple roles, including the following:

1. Interviewing incoming students and family members in the native language in order to (a) become knowledgeable about significant events in the students' lives that may affect their learning (e.g., experiencing war or loss of close family members), (b) record past schooling experiences and performance, (c) identify any potential special needs (e.g., gifted and talented or learning disabled), and (d) interpret any school records brought by families.

2. Assessing students in the native language for their content-area knowledge.

3. Assessing students' fluency in English (orally, as readers, and in writing).

4. Providing staff development to district faculty and staff on a variety of issues (e.g., linguistic features of the native language that may appear in students' oral and written language; cultural nuances of various ethnic groups in the district; and home culture medical practices that may be unfamiliar to faculty and staff).

5. Locating resources for faculty and staff (e.g., background information on a particular country, language, or culture; books in the native language or bilingual books and other print and technological resources; and speakers).

6. Training and overseeing other district personnel who administer LEP census tools (e.g., the BSM or BINL).

7. Collecting assessment data for program evaluation purposes.

8. Providing guidance to teachers who have questions about students.

See Figure 6–5 for an overview of the role of placement centers.

We have found that the services provided by placement centers are usually implemented well and of tremendous benefit to other district personnel, particularly teachers. Because the centers are staffed by knowledgeable and skilled educators, they are less likely to place students inappropriately, a phenomenon that is all too frequent (e.g., 10 year-old students being placed in a first-grade class or eleventh graders who have taken calculus in their home country being placed in basic math classes).

Misplacement of students can have a profound and negative impact on students. Sometimes, the misplacement is grounded in misuse of the term bilingual. This word means many things to different people. Although the dictionary defines it as "able to speak two languages with equal skill" (*The American Heritage Dictionary* 1985), one of its most popular (and inaccurate) meanings in the United States is to use it in reference to a person who is not fluent in English. This can have serious consequences when it leads to the inappropriate placement of students, as the following incident illustrates. One of us conducted a bilingual/ESOL review of a school district that served large numbers of LEP students. This review involved visiting several bilingual classes, most of which were being taught in Spanish and English. Some of the students were of Asian descent and the reviewers assumed that they were fluent Spanish speakers who were descendants of immigrants to Latin American countries. In conversations with the teachers, however, it became apparent that none of these students spoke Spanish. They had been placed in the bilingual class because they were LEP. The staff did not at first see the inappropriateness of this placement, stating, "But they're learning Spanish, also." The person who had conducted the initial assessment had been a monolingual speaker of English who did not have a teaching certificate. It is likely that this situation would not have occurred had the district established a placement center and staffed it with knowledgeable, skilled assessors.

Figure 6–5
The Role of Placement Centers

- Interview students and family members in the L1
- Assess students in the L1 for subject-matter knowledge
- Assess students' fluency in English (oral and literacy)
- Act as resource to faculty and staff
- Provide staff development
- Locate resources for faculty and staff
- Train and oversee those who administer LEP census tools
- Collect program evaluation data

Scenario

In Coldwater Unified School District, a placement center was established several years ago after administrators and teachers complained repeatedly about the difficulties they had in assessing students and making appropriate placement decisions, because they had limited resources. The district decided to centralize intake and placement procedures. The placement center is staffed by educators who are knowledgeable about language acquisition and development, and fluent in the dominant languages spoken in the district (Spanish, Vietnamese, Laotian, Urdu). They are able to easily assess newcomers' academic background and achievement, and special needs and interests through the native language. In the case of other languages, translators are available. All modes of English language fluency are also assessed by a fluent English speaker. These data are then integrated and used for placement recommendations.

Brief reports containing pertinent information about the incoming students are also sent to the receiving schools. In this way, teachers are provided with important information at the beginning of their interactions with the newcomers, and students are more appropriately placed than had often been the case before the placement center was established. Critical issues that they are better able to address include the following: (1) placing students in appropriate academic classes that challenge them, (2) identifying students who may have special learning needs so that teachers and other employees are alerted at an early stage to potential learning problems, and are able to make appropriate adjustments in instruction, and(3) providing teachers with more useful information than a score on a test can provide.

Assessment Myth #5: Our teachers have to administer state-mandated tests each year. We can't possibly ask them to do even more assessments, which take valuable time away from teaching and learning.

Reality: As these norm-referenced, standardized assessments rarely help teachers make instructional decisions, it is critical that teachers conduct appropriate formal and informal assessments that are tied to their instructional goals.

Background/Overview

While there is more and more legislation mandating large-scale testing for accountability purposes, there is also a growing awareness on the part of teachers of the usefulness of learner-centered, ongoing assessments that can be conducted as a normal part of the schoolday. Rather than making instructional decisions based on a scope and sequence in a teacher's manual, teachers are beginning to use individualized, meaningful assessment procedures to help them accomplish the following: (1) determine what students can do; (2) establish students' learning strategies, skills, and processes; (3) make instructional decisions; and (4) decide how to flexibly group students for instruction (e.g., Clay 1993; Fountas & Pinnell 1996). Teachers are beginning to recognize the need to be skilled observers of learners, applying this skill throughout the day and using the observations to make instructional decisions, at the moment and for the future (e.g., Baskwill & Whitman 1988; Goodman 1985; Navarrete et al. 1990). When assessing L2 learners, it is important to assess them in all language modalities (listening, speaking, reading, writing) and to take into account the multiple purposes for which we need and use language (e.g., to inform and advise, command, express needs and wishes, gain information, express feelings, persuade, amuse or entertain, clarify thinking, and establish, explore, and maintain relationships). It is also important to invite students and their caregivers to assess the students' performance, progress, needs, and goals (see Barrs et al. 1989; Farr & Tone 1998; Woodward 1994). The following list includes some learner-centered assessment procedures and tools that we have found helpful. Many of them are described in detail in several publications (e.g., Kemp 1987; Rhodes 1993; Farr & Tone 1998). See Figure 6–6 for an overview of features of learner-centered assessment.

Figure 6–6
Features of Learner-Centered Assessment

- ➡ Is ongoing and continuous
- ➡ Determines what students can do linguistically and academically
- ➡ Identifies students' learning strategies, skills, and processes
- ➡ Facilitates sound instructional decision making
- ➡ Assists in grouping students for instruction
- ➡ Addresses all language modalities (listening, speaking, reading, writing)
- ➡ Incorporates student self-assessment
- ➡ Invites parent assessment of students

For Assessing Listening

→ Hands-on tasks (e.g., "Take the book and put it on the bookshelf by the door.")

→ Draw in response to oral directions (e.g., "Draw a square and put a star in the middle.")

For Assessing Speaking

Audiotapes and videotapes: Periodically tape record a student's oral language in a variety of contexts (e.g., giving directions for making a puppet, reporting on a science experiment, telling a family story). Make sure that each entry is dated. It is also possible to tape record or videotape any of the assessment techniques that follow.

→ Tasks (e.g., "Tell us how to make a favorite dish; explain photosynthesis; call and find out how much 5 pounds of rice costs.")

→ Reading aloud a familiar text: Pay attention to fluency, including attention to punctuation marks and intonation.

→ Telling a story/riddle/rhyme/joke (a more complex linguistic task)

→ Dialogues and open-ended scenarios: Students are provided with conversation information (e.g., background information on their character and the situation) and have to create their own sketches.

→ Group discussions

→ Presentations/reports

→ Interviews

→ Observations: Observe students as they interact with their peers, in the classroom, on the playground, in the cafeteria, in special classes, such as PE.

→ Speaking rubrics and rating scales

→ Self-assessments

For Assessing Reading

→ Running records (Clay 1993)

→ Observation Survey Tasks (e.g., concepts about print, word recognition) (Clay 1993)

→ Miscue analysis (including retellings) (Goodman, Watson & Burke 1987)

→ Retrospective miscue analysis (Goodman & Marek 1996)

→ Cloze procedures

→ Sequencing texts (a sentence, several sentences, longer texts)

→ Periodic audiotapes or videotapes of learners reading familiar and unfamiliar texts

→ Questionnaires/surveys

→ Reading rubrics and rating scales

→ Reading checklists

➡ Surveys (e.g., Burke Reading Inventory)

➡ Interviews (of learners and caregivers)

➡ Observational/anecdotal records (e.g., while observing; in reading conferences)

➡ Lists/logs (e.g., of books read)

➡ Reading response journals

➡ Self-assessments

For Assessing Writing

➡ Dictation (word, sentence, etc.)

➡ Writing samples collected over time (different genres)

➡ Drafts of a particular piece

➡ Writing checklists

➡ Writing rubrics and rating scales (sometimes referred to as analytic scoring of writing)

➡ Lists/logs (e.g., of writing skills taught)

➡ Holistic scoring of writing

➡ Periodic videotapes of students' writing

➡ Observational/anecdotal records

➡ Interviews (of students and caregivers)

➡ Self-assessments

See Figure 6–7 for an overview of learner-centered assessment tools.

States and school districts are also exploring the role of portfolio assessment in assessing students' progress and needs (see Graves & Sunstein 1992; Pierce & O' Malley 1992; Tierney, Carter & Desai 1991; Valencia 1998). In portfolios, artifacts that reflect each student's learning are collected over the course of a year. These portfolios may include audio- or videotapes, pieces of writing, checklists, and other documents that reveal what the learner has been involved with over a period of time, accomplishments, and future directions. It is common for the learner to engage in some form of self-assessment, and this is included in the portfolio, often in the form of a reflective letter to readers of the portfolio. In some cases, parents and caregivers also provide input, for example, in the course of an interview in which they comment on and inform the teacher about a child's learning strategies and preferred activities at home (see Barrs et al. 1989).

Until recently, Title I regulations required that districts report norm-referenced, standardized testing results, but under pressure from the education community, this requirement was dropped from the most recent regulations governing the Elementary and Secondary Education Act. By releasing districts from certain constraints, educators now have a significant opportunity to develop and implement assessment designs that address the needs of students and classroom teachers, as well as the needs of districts for accountability.

Figure 6–7
Learner-Centered Assessment Tools and Procedures for Use with L2 Learners

	TO ASSESS LISTENING	TO ASSESS SPEAKING	TO ASSESS READING	TO ASSESS WRITING
Audiotapes and videotapes	x	x	x	x
Checklists	x	x	x	x
Cloze procedures		x	x	
Dialogues and open-ended scenarios		x		
Dictations				x
Drawing	x		x	
Group discussions		x	x	x
Hands-on tasks	x	x		x
Holistic scoring				x
Interviews	x	x	x	x
Lists/logs	x	x	x	x
Miscue analysis		x	x	
Clay's Observation Survey Tasks			x	
Observational records	x	x	x	x
Presentations/reports		x		x
Questionnaires and surveys	x	x	x	x
Reading aloud		x	x	
Reading response journals			x	x
Retrospective miscue analysis		x	x	
Rubrics and rating scales	x	x	x	x
Running records			x	
Self-assessments	x	x	x	x
Sequencing texts			x	
Surveys and interviews	x	x	x	x
Telling a story/riddle/rhyme/joke		x		
Writing samples, including drafts				x

Scenario

The primary grade faculty at a rural school, Los Arboles Elementary School, realized that they needed to examine the assessment practices that they used with all students, particularly LEP students. Although students were assessed at regular intervals throughout the year, usually using formal measures, the assessments rarely helped teachers make appropriate instructional decisions. For example, legal requirements dictated that the district administer a language dominance test in order to establish which students were LEP. The district used the Bilingual Syntax Measure (BSM), an oral language test that was administered by a central office employee at the beginning and end of the year; the results rarely filtered back to the teachers. Through discussing how little they knew about their LEP students, the faculty and staff realized that they needed to overhaul what they assessed and how they assessed students' progress.

When the teachers shared their concerns with the principal, it became evident that the entire school needed to be involved. As a consequence, this quest on the part of the primary teachers led to an invigorating year-long process for the entire school. The principal arranged for the entire instructional faculty and staff to meet for a full day with the district's language and literacy specialist. Under her guidance, the principal, teachers, and instructional aides brainstormed school-wide goals in language and literacy. They decided to begin there, because all other content areas rely heavily on language and literacy, and they agreed to work on other curricular areas, such as science, mathematics, and social studies, once they had established an effective and meaningful assessment plan for language and literacy. While brainstorming, they delved into the English/Language Arts standards developed by their own district (which they found to be rather dated) and professional organizations (i.e., National Council of Teachers of English & International Reading Association 1996; Teachers of English to Speakers of Other Languages 1997).

After agreeing on some key schoolwide goals (e.g., that all students be able to express and back up an opinion orally, write effectively across genres, and read for meaning), grade-level groups then met to explore how these goals would look at their particular grade level, taking into account that there is considerable developmental variation across students in any grade. The group ended the day with the district's language and literacy specialist providing an orientation to a wide range of learner-centered assessment tools and techniques, including checklists, observational strategies, interviews, and surveys. For the remainder of the semester, the teachers worked with and revised existing tools, and developed new procedures that assisted them in their classrooms. They also met on a monthly basis for in-depth progress reports and the refinement of group goals and responsibilities. At the end of the school year, when the entire instructional faculty and staff met one last time with the district's language and literacy specialist, they selected several assessment procedures for full adoption by the school the following year:

1. *Running records for students who were beginning to read.*

2. *Modified miscue analysis for struggling upper grade readers.*

3. *Clay's other observation survey tasks for students who were not yet reading (e.g., letter identification, concepts about print, dictation).*

4. Tape recorded oral samples of L2 learners, taken monthly.

5. A two-part writing portfolio for which both students and teachers selected writing samples from across genres.

6. Reading and writing rubrics that would be completed twice a semester.

7. A language and literacy survey that students would complete at the beginning of the year, mid-year, and end of the year. Teachers or instructional aides would administer this orally to newcomer students.

8. Teacher observation records. Teachers used a variety of strategies for collecting and storing the data, including peel-off address labels, index cards, and Post-its (Samway 1994). The faculty decided to collect these data on each child once or twice a month until they became more skilled, when they hoped to record notes on each child at least once a week.

9. Interviews with caregivers. The school decided to use the Primary Language Record (Barrs et al. 1989) for this activity.

Assessment Myth #6: Given limited resources, it's OK for districts to assess L2 students suspected of having a learning handicap in English only.

Reality: PL 94-142 requires that districts assess L2 students suspected of having a handicapping condition in their native language. Communication with parents must also be conducted in such a way that parents understand; for some parents, this may mean communication in their native language.

Background/Overview

Historically, a disproportionate number of LEP students have been placed in special education classes, which Cummins has characterized as "institutionalized racism" (1991). For example, according to Cummins, until the 1970s there were three times as many Hispanic students designated as educable mentally retarded than would be expected, given their numbers in the general population. Much of the blame for this state of affairs can be attributed to culturally and linguistically biased psychoeducational tests (e.g., the WISC-R), which are frequently used to determine special education status, and tests being administered in a nonnative language. In some cases, students are thought to be sufficiently fluent in English to be assessed in English. Frequently, this appearance of fluency in English is determined solely by the students' skill in communicating in contextualized, face-to-face oral interactions; however, it takes many years for most L2 learners to achieve fluent command of more decontextualized language, such as one finds on reading tests.

Lawsuits in the United States (e.g., *Diana v. California State Board of Education* 1970) led to the development of policies that recognize that students from non-English-speaking backgrounds must be assessed in their native or dominant language. This requirement was incorporated into Public Law (PL) 94-142, which guarantees an appropriate education to all children with handicapping conditions. In the past 20 years, the field of bilingual education has grown, and one consequence has been a marked reduction in the number of language minority students classified as educable mentally retarded. However, according to Cummins (1991), there has been a marked increase in the number of language minority students classified as learning disabled.

In addition to requiring that assessment of students suspected of having a handicapping condition must be conducted in the primary or dominant language, PL 94-142 also requires the following: (1) Assessment instruments must be valid for their intended purpose, (2) test administrators should be trained personnel who are knowledgeable about the linguistic and cultural backgrounds of the students being tested, and (3) program placement should be tailored to the needs of the students classified as having a handicapping condition (Samuda 1991).

Scenario

"He really is a handful," remarks Susana Majors, a second-grade teacher, to her colleagues in the lunchroom. "He's hyper so much of the time that I end up totally exhausted by the end of the day. I wonder if he's ADD [Attention Deficit Disorder]?" The other teachers nod their heads in sympathy as Susana goes on to describe how Javier, a new student to the school, moves around the classroom constantly, avoids working on his own, and shows disrespect by not looking at her when she is reprimanding him. One of her colleagues urges her to refer him for special testing.

Two weeks later, the school psychologist sends a letter to Javier's parents, informing them in English that she will be testing Javier and to contact her if they have any concerns or questions. She does not hear back from his family. One week later, she picks up Javier from his classroom and administers a battery of psychoeducational tests in English. He is reluctant to cooperate, fidgets with the testing materials, hardly speaks, and seems very preoccupied. The psychologist considers abandoning the testing, but perseveres. The test scores indicate that Javier is borderline educable mentally retarded and he is placed with a self-contained special education teacher.

Within days, this teacher, Andrea Anderson, is questioning the appropriateness of Javier's placement. She speaks Spanish, which Javier finds out rather quickly and then uses consistently with her. She contacts his parents and discovers that he did not attend kindergarten in the United States and was in a Spanish-English bilingual first-grade class the previous year, in another state. According to his parents, they hadn't been able to bring his school records with them because they left so quickly. They remembered receiving letters from the district, but didn't read English and had no idea what the letter was referring to.

In the classroom, Andrea sees that Javier is an alert, engaged, sociable, intelligent child when he understands what is going on. From living and working in a Latin American country, she understands that his lack of eye contact when being reprimanded is ac-

tually a sign of respect. Armed with these data, Andrea Anderson approaches her principal about a more appropriate placement. With the agreement of his parents, Javier is placed in another school in the district where there is an ESOL teacher who works closely with the primary teachers, in addition to providing pull-out instruction to L2 students. Javier thrives in this new environment.

Chapter 7

Programming Myths

Programming Myth #1: Research is unequivocal about the most effective program for L2 students.

Reality: No single program fits all students.

hard to
collaborate
w/ others & r
get new ideas

Background/Overview

For years, the $64,000 question has been, "Does bilingual education work?" Attempts to compare bilingual programs with other programs serving L2 students have produced seemingly conflicting answers. Ramirez et al. (1991) point out one severe problem with program comparison research. Program designs vary so widely from site to site that a bilingual education program in one district may look nothing like a program also designated as bilingual in a neighboring district. Moreover, the differences between program designs and classifications can be so great that what might be classified as a bilingual program in one state would not even come close to meeting the minimum requirements of a bilingual program in another state. Even though the name may be the same, the basic program design is not. While in some cases it may be like comparing apples and oranges, in other cases it may be like comparing Golden Delicious apples and Granny Smiths.

Collier's (1989) review of the research may help to explain why the results from research examining program effectiveness for language minority students seem to be so contradictory. The complexity of the interactions between language learning and academic achievement described by Collier's synthesis helps to explain the difficulties encountered when conducting research on the effectiveness of programs designed for L2 students.

Program comparisons are rarely easy. In the case of programs for L2 students, the sociopolitical context of the United States often makes comparisons excruciatingly difficult, as arguments for and against the use of students' native languages for instructional purposes rage against a backdrop of strongly held values and beliefs. In fact, such comparisons have often produced more heat than light because political, social, and economic agendas drive the formation of research questions and, ultimately, the interpretation of results.

Sociopolitical context aside, much of the research evaluating programs for L2 students appears to suffer from three serious shortcomings: (1) It obscures the striking

70

diversity of programs in design and quality (including the availability of resources, materials, and trained staff), (2) it obscures the way in which language is actually used for instructional purposes, and (3) it obscures the linguistic, social, and academic characteristics of students (Hakuta & Gould 1987). In short, as Crawford (1989) points out:

> Educators are beginning to recognize the theoretical fallacies of gauging "program effectiveness" narrowly defined ... [They are beginning to recognize that] research focusing on bottom-line results, especially when measured with imperfect instruments makes for crude science. (p. 88)

These criticisms notwithstanding, schools need to be able to make decisions about program design and implementation. With that need in mind, we will examine four of the most widely cited studies of program effectiveness: (1) the Baker and de Kanter Report (1981, 1983), (2) Willig's (1985) meta-analysis, (3) the National Longitudinal Study (Ramirez et al. 1991), and (4) Collier's (1992) synthesis of studies examining long-term data on the academic achievement of language minority students. We begin by defining several of the program terms that are examined in effectiveness studies. It must be noted that definitions of these program types are general definitions. In reality, the way in which each program type operates may vary dramatically from district to district and from school to school.

Different Types of Programs

The term *bilingual education* is used to describe a number of educational approaches using English and another language for instruction. True bilingual programs are those that include the following: (1) use of the students' dominant language (usually the language used in the home), (2) teaching of content-area subjects through both the dominant and target languages, and (3) teaching the target language (the language to be learned, which in the case of LEP students in the United States is English). Using this definition, it is easy to see how bilingual programs can be designed and developed for both LEP and monolingual English speakers. In the case of LEP students, for example, bilingual education includes teaching English as a Second Language (ESL) or, as it is called in some parts of the country, teaching English to Speakers of Other Languages (ESOL), as well as teaching content such as science, social studies, and mathematics using either English and/or the native language of students.

Two-way bilingual education programs are a relatively new type of program design in the United States. In these programs, language minority students work together academically with language majority students (i.e., native English speakers), with both groups of students learning language and content through two languages. Such programs are thought to lessen the social distance and unequal social status that is often found between minority and majority language students.

It is important to note that every bilingual program includes an ESOL component, as many people are under the misunderstanding that all teaching

[handwritten margin notes: "doesn't agree w/ past knowledge" and "require teacher to be language proficient?"]

in bilingual programs is in the native language. Within the broad definition of bilingual education, however, there is tremendous variation in the degree to which the native language is used in the classroom. In some cases, the native language is used almost exclusively for content-area teaching, with English-medium instruction being introduced gradually. In other cases, English is used from the outset for one or two content-area classes, with the native language used in the remaining classes.

Structured immersion programs are usually defined as programs that use the target language (English, in the case of LEP students) for most instruction. Teachers in these programs are bilingual. They understand and accept their students' use of the native language, but generally teach in and respond to students in the target language. Interestingly, this use of the native language parallels the degree of use found in some bilingual education models used in the United States, so even though these programs technically would not be considered bilingual programs, they sometimes function in precisely the same way that certain bilingual program models do.

ESOL programs are also referred to as *ESL* programs. The teachers are not necessarily bilingual, and all instruction is in English. L2 students are usually pulled out of their regular education classrooms once or twice a day for specialized instruction. These classes focus on developing language, but increasingly ESOL teachers are integrating language and content instruction. Sometimes, the ESOL teacher collaborates with classroom teachers in a push-in model; in these cases, the ESOL teacher plans with and teaches alongside the classroom teacher.

Sheltered English, content-based ESOL, and *Specially Designed Academic Instruction in English (SDAIE)* programs are those that offer content classes designed specifically for LEP students. They parallel content classes found in the general curriculum, but employ teaching methods that incorporate the development of both language and content. Courses may be team-taught by a content specialist and an ESOL specialist, or they may be taught by an ESOL teacher. Teachers are not necessarily bilingual, as is the case in both bilingual education and structured immersion programs. In many cases, students in these classes speak a variety of native languages.

Submersion programs are usually called "*sink or swim*" programs. In such cases, LEP students are placed in "mainstream" or regular education classes throughout most of the schoolday. They may receive some form of special assistance by way of ESOL classes or one-on-one tutorial support on a pull-out basis, but in large part, are left to fend for themselves.

Four Studies of Program Effectiveness

1. The Baker and de Kanter Report

The Baker and de Kanter Report was designed to determine whether bilingual education was uniformly effective. The initial Baker and de Kanter Report *need for a Quality study*

(1981) was a widely circulated draft of a study conducted by the Department of Education, Office of Planning and Budget. The study reviewed over 300 studies, half of which were primary evaluations of actual programs for LEP students. Of these 300, all but twenty-eight were discarded because of design flaws such as failure to adjust for preexisting conditions between experimental groups, failure to randomly assign students to "treatment groups," or the use of grade-equivalent scores (Crawford 1989).

Using a narrative review technique, in the majority of the twenty-eight evaluations, the researchers found that differences in student performance were too small to be statistically significant when bilingual education was compared with submersion or "sink or swim" instruction. Among the studies that showed one method to be superior, the score was split about evenly between the two— bilingual education and submersion. Baker and de Kanter argued that bilingual education and submersion programs were less effective than either ESOL or structured immersion programs. However, this argument appears to have been made on the basis of one unpublished study of a kindergarten program in McAllen, Texas, which the researchers labeled as a "modified immersion program," even though it included an hour of daily Spanish instruction. *not good study*

dep. on student ("rise to the occasion")

2. *Willig's Meta-analysis*

On the heels of the Baker and de Kanter Report came Willig's (1985) meta-analysis. Willig reanalyzed twenty-three of the twenty-eight studies reviewed by Baker and de Kanter. She eliminated foreign and nonprimary studies. By using more sophisticated statistical procedures, Willig was able to examine differences between programs that were too small to be statistically significant in individual studies. She was also able to adjust for 183 variables that Baker and de Kanter had not taken into account, including student and teacher characteristics, instructional methods, and the language of the achievement tests used. Contrary to the finding of Baker and de Kanter, Willig's meta-analysis consistently produced small-to-moderate differences favoring bilingual education.

3. *National Longitudinal Study (The Ramirez Report)*

Willig's findings were supported in 1991 by a Department of Education study of three program alternatives: structured English immersion, early-exit transitional bilingual education, and late-exit transitional bilingual education. A massive undertaking, the study collected longitudinal data over a period of 4 years from over 2,300 Spanish-speaking students in 554 classrooms (K–6) in New York, New Jersey, Florida, Texas, and California. The study, known informally as the Ramirez Report (after the study's primary author), concluded that LEP students in bilingual programs improved in mathematics, English language, and reading in English as fast or faster than the general population (Congressional Quarterly Researcher 1993). In addition, the study concluded that Latin American students who had received at least 40% of their instruction in Spanish throughout elementary school (also known as "late-exit" students) appeared to *good to use native lang.*

have better prospects of catching up academically in English with their native English-speaking peers than did similar students who had received all of their instruction in English or had been exited to an all-English program in the early grades (around grade 2), also known as "early exit" students. Students in the early-exit bilingual and structured English immersion programs performed at about the same level. In his review of the Ramirez Report, Cziko (1992) states:

> The impressive growth rates shown by students in late-exit bilingual programs suggest that giving the native language a much more important role than is typically done in bilingual programs may enable these at-risk students to achieve at levels comparable to those of majority students. (p. 12)

In discussing the results of the Ramirez Report, it is also necessary to report that, upon its conclusion, the Department of Education commissioned the National Academy of Sciences (NAS) to critique it. The study had been long-anticipated and much-speculated about. Given the political context surrounding bilingual education, every avenue was pursued to ensure that the findings were sound. This critique, although critical of the study's methodology, concluded that the "elements of positive relationships that are consistent with empirical results from other studies . . . support the theory underlying native language instruction in bilingual education" (Meyer & Feinberg 1992, 105).

If inst. is always in native language — does the need eventually to learn English?

4. *Collier's Synthesis of Long-term Achievement*

The final study of program effectiveness that we examine is a synthesis of studies that examined language minority students' achievement over a period of 4 or more years. This synthesis examined one program variable: the use of a minority language for student achievement. In other words, Collier examined the effect of instruction in the native language on students' academic achievement. Her review of seventeen studies conducted in the 1980s was limited to those studies that reported results in terms of normal curve equivalents (NCEs) on standardized tests. This permitted an investigation of the performance of language minority students when compared with the national average for native English-speaking students who had taken the same tests. However, unlike the Ramirez Study, Collier included two-way bilingual programs in her analysis, along with late-exit bilingual, early-exit bilingual, structured immersion, and ESOL programs.

What are goals for L2 students?

Collier (1992) reports that the general patterns of achievement for language minority students show that the greater the amount of native language instruction provided to language minority students (combined with balanced support in English), the higher they are able to achieve academically in English in each succeeding year. That is, these language minority students do better than matched groups of students who have been schooled only in English. Collier goes on to conclude that the two-way and late-exit bilingual programs appear to be the most promising in helping language minority students succeed academically. She also found that early-exit bilingual programs provide support to students, but may not be as successful in the long run.

Where Does the Research on Program Effectiveness Leave Us?

Given the research evidence, many educators and policymakers have now come to the conclusion that bilingual education programs (and, in particular, the use of the native language) are effective in helping students learn English and academic content (ASCD Panel on Bilingual Education 1987; Collier 1992; Cziko 1992; General Accounting Office [GAO] 1987; Hakuta & Gould 1987; Ramirez et al. 1991; Willig 1985). Even Keith Baker, whose 1981 report with Adriana de Kanter came down squarely in favor of English immersion and ESOL approaches, has since stated that transitional bilingual approaches appear to work more effectively than English-only approaches (Baker 1993).

However, many researchers are also convinced that the questions, "Does bilingual education work?" and "Does bilingual education work better than any other alternative design?" are the wrong questions to be asking (Cziko 1992; Gándara & Merino 1993). If we disengage ourselves from these two questions, and turn instead to the question, "What strategies or program design features help LEP students achieve academically in U.S. schools?" we can begin to uncover more concrete solutions to the challenges that schools face.

Legal Considerations

In *Teresa P. v. Berkeley Unified School District* (1989), a suit was brought by a group representing LEP students who argued that native language instruction by teachers trained in this work should be offered to all LEP students in the district. At the time, the district offered an English-based program and a native language instructional program that was primarily geared to Spanish speakers. The plaintiffs argued that all students should have access to full-fledged native language instructional programs. Given that there were thirty-eight language groups in the district, the federal district court noted that it was unlikely that Berkeley could find teachers at all grade levels who spoke and could teach in such a large number of languages. The court also accepted evidence showing that on state tests, LEP students from Berkeley schools did as well as or better than students in schools with native language instructional models; the court ruled that "the educational theories on which [the district's] programs are grounded are manifestly as sound as any theory identified by the plaintiffs" (Stewart 1993, 44). For districts serving students from many language groups, the court's decision was significant because it implied that schools would not be required to provide native language instructional programs as long as they could show that students who were served by other types of programs performed as well as their peers in bilingual education programs.

Strong assessment?

Programming Myth #2: Researchers can't agree on what's the most effective program for L2 students.

Reality: There is considerable agreement over indicators of effective schooling for L2 students.

Background/Overview

The literature on effective programs offers several clues about program design features that serve L2 students well from early childhood (Pease-Alvarez, Garcia & Espinosa 1991) to the secondary level (Lucas, Henze & Donato 1990; Minicucci & Olsen 1992), and from bilingual programs (Collier 1992; Lindholm 1987; Ramirez et al. 1991) to programs that primarily provide instruction through English (Arlington Public Schools 1993; Crandall 1987; Snow, Met & Genesee 1989; Tikunoff et al. 1991). This literature has isolated several indicators of effective schooling for L2 students. (See Figure 7–1 for features of effective programs.)

Indicator 1: High Expectations for LEP and Language Minority Students

Across the board, studies of programs for LEP and language minority students show that those programs that are considered effective hold high expectations that students can achieve academic success (Collier, Henze & Donato 1992; Lucas et al. 1990; Pease-Alvarez, Garcia & Espinosa 1991; Tikunoff et al. 1991). This is true regardless of program type. Full access to a wide variety of language-sensitive curricular offerings (rather than access to only the most basic-level content classes) is one demonstration of high expectations (Minicucci & Olsen 1992). Holding LEP students to the same standards of achievement as monolingual English speakers is another.

Indicator 2: Active Use of Language/Integration of Language Development with Content-Area Development

Because language development is facilitated in environments where language is used for real communication purposes (rather than drill and practice), effective programs feature instructional designs that place students in proximity to each other and demand that they interact to complete meaningful tasks (Tikunoff et al. 1991; Lindholm 1987). English language development is integrated with content instruction, rather than being taught in isolation (Arlington Public Schools 1993; Crandall 1987; Snow, Met & Genesee 1989).

Indicator 3: Support for Concept Development Through the L1

Even in programs that use English as the language of instruction, the use of students' native languages has been found to be an indicator of program effectiveness (Tikunoff et al. 1991). In such cases, teachers allow students who understand what is being asked, but cannot respond yet in English, to respond in the native language. Teachers who are not fluent in the students' native languages turn to others for translation, and use this interaction to develop the English behind the concept under study. In studies of bilingual programs, the most effective programs are those that provide consistent, long-term use of the native language for concept development (Collier 1992; Ramirez et al. 1991).

Figure 7–1
Features of Effective Programs for L2 Learners

- High expectations are held for L2 students.
- Language and subject matter development are integrated.
- Concept development in the L1 is supported.
- Comprehensive staff development for all faculty and staff is provided.
- The entire school environment supports L2 learners.
- Active support from school leaders.

Indicator 4: Comprehensive Training for Teachers and Staff

The need for comprehensive training for teachers and staff serving LEP students cannot be overstated. Programs that include *all* staff, not just program teachers, contribute greatly to program success (Lucas, Henze & Donato 1990; McKeon & Malarz 1991; Tikunoff et al. 1991).

Indicator 5: Instructional Leadership

Active support from school leaders such as principals and other administrators is evident in environments that typify effective programs (Lindholm 1987; Lucas, Henze & Donato 1990; Tikunoff et al. 1991). Effective programs are characterized by the presence of instructional leaders who assume responsibility for planning, coordinating, and administering the program for L2 students (McKeon & Malarz 1991; Tikunoff et al. 1991).

Indicator 6: Supportive Whole-School Contexts

Most effective programs for LEP students are part of a larger, whole-school environment that is organized to support and value the special resources, abilities, and needs of L2 students (Lindholm 1897; Lucas, Henze & Donato 1990; Tikunoff et al. 1991). Often, the school has adopted new ways of extending learning beyond the traditional schoolday or schoolyear by employing extended or year-round programming (Gandara & Fish 1994). Schools may also extend learning beyond the walls of the classroom, finding ways to reach out to parents and the larger community as learning resources and strong allies (Guthrie 1985; Lindholm 1987; Tikunoff et al. 1991).

Scenario

A mid-sized school district had undergone a state department of education review. Overall, the review was positive, but the district was asked to provide more support in the native language for L2 students. The district did not have large numbers of students from any one language group at a given grade level or teachers who could speak a language spoken by the LEP students. Each school was asked to address the issue in a way that would work best for their L2 students. At Glendale Elementary school, teachers, instructional aides, clerical workers, and the principal volunteered to prepare a draft plan, which was approved by the entire school faculty and staff, as well as the school district. Glendale School succeeded in implementing the following actions:

1. *Purchasing books, films, and other media in languages spoken by L2 students, as well as books written in English that reflected the cultures of the student body, and placing them in the school library and all classrooms. This involved contacting a regional technical assistance center and professors at the local university for references, visiting ethnic bookstores and book distributors that specialize in primary language literature, and writing small grants to purchase materials.*

2. *Providing staff development to teachers and instructional aides that focused on why and how to encourage students to write in whichever language they were most comfortable, whether in journals, stories, or reports. The rationale for this recommendation/action was grounded in the understanding that, although teachers would often not be able to read the text, it was important for students to have the freedom to express their ideas in the most accessible way. Also, it recognized that the desire to make a message accessible to others in the class would lead to spontaneous translation on the part of the writer or peers. This experience of seeing texts written in a language other than English would also be a way of allowing the least fluent English speakers opportunities to be experts and highly valued members of the class, and, in the process, helping everyone to develop respect for diversity, to which the school was committed.*

3. *Establishing a book group for the faculty and staff, which began meeting on a biweekly basis to discuss multicultural and bilingual children's literature.*

4. *Exploring ways in which themes and learning experiences could take on a more dynamic cross-cultural flavor.*

5. *Contacting nonnative English-speaking community resources whc could come into the classrooms to share their expertise.*

6. *Writing a family literacy federal grant proposal in order to enhance the literacy development of parents through family stories and children's literature, and to become more knowledgeable about the community.*

The school realized that it needed to make a greater effort to know much more about its students' backgrounds, customs, and experiences. They understood that, for the most part, the content of the schoolday was often very foreign to its LEP students, particularly those who were more recent arrivals. Through discussion, they understood that by skewing the curriculum so far from students' experiences they were in danger of undermining the learning of their students. They realized that it made sense to begin with the knowledge that students had already accumulated in their already rich lives, to build on that, and to enhance the wealth of knowledge by introducing students to different experiences. This symbiotic rela-

tionship between experience and learning had not been fully addressed by any of the class-rooms in the past. In fact, about the only times that students were encouraged to explore or draw upon their roots and culture were at holiday times, which received rather superficial treatment of issues that are considerably more complex and subtle than ethnic foods, traditional clothing (often referred to as "costumes"), and dance capture.

A group of fourth-grade teachers, who were particularly interested in the family literacy project, began to work closely with the ESOL teacher who taught English to adult family members. The adult students had been writing books about family stories. The fourth-grade teachers decided to invite their students to do the same, which they integrated into their writers' workshops. Students became very enthusiastic (and quite skilled) writers, and the fact that they knew that other people were reading them, and learning English through them, appeared to enhance their enthusiasm. Books were written in English; many were translated by L2 students so that the adult ESOL class had access to bilingual versions. The project was so successful that the school made copies of the books (those written by the adults as well as by the children) and placed them in the primary classrooms, where they were devoured. The younger children took great pleasure in reading stories written by their siblings and parents, particularly those in which they were featured.

Programming Myth #3: Newcomer centers are no longer a legal program option for L2 students.

Reality: Newcomer centers are not illegal. However, districts must ensure that students placed in such centers are not segregated solely on the basis of race or ethnic group. *What about language?*

Background/Overview

Newcomer centers or schools typically serve immigrant students as they enter the district, temporarily separating them from the general school population for special instruction in English, content-area instruction in either the native language or sheltered English (SDAIE) classes, and help in making the transition to a new culture. Sometimes, newcomer schools serve students for half a day and students spend the remainder of the schoolday in their home school. In other newcomer schools, L2 students attend for the entire day. Some newcomer centers are housed in an already established school, whereas others are self-contained schools. Newcomer centers or schools may serve all grades, but it is more common to find schools designed for elementary, secondary (7–12), or high school students.

Concern about the potential segregation of LEP and language minority students led the Office of Civil Rights (OCR) to investigate one of the newcomer schools for possible violations of the Civil Rights Act of 1964. Although the OCR review of this newcomer school found that the school did not segregate students solely on the basis of race or ethnic group, OCR had serious reservations about the existence of such a program at a separate site (Stewart 1993). However, OCR found the district in compliance with Title VI of the Civil Rights Act of 1964 based on several extenuating circumstances, which OCR cited in a memorandum of December 4, 1990 (Friedlander 1991):

- The district was not operating under an order to desegregate its schools.
- Enrollment in the newcomer school was ~~voluntary.~~
- The newcomer school was multiethnic, multiracial, and multilinguistic.
- Attendance at the school was limited to no more than 1 year; students transferred to their home schools in less than a year.
- Students attended the school based on their need for both language services and assistance in adjusting to American culture.
- The facilities and range of courses and extracurricular activities were comparable to those at the district's other schools.

This OCR finding provides valuable guidelines to schools and districts that are interested in implementing a newcomer school program option. In fact, these guidelines may help to determine at the outset whether such a program would be a viable option in a given district.

How do students like this?

Scenario

Several years ago, a medium-sized urban school district established a newcomer high school. It came about in response to the crisis posed by an influx of adolescent refugees from war-torn countries. Most of the newcomers did not know English when they entered high school and were completely unfamiliar with an American school experience. Unable to understand the content of their academic classes, and lacking familiarity with school procedures and rituals, the L2 students were often marginalized, and many dropped out of school.

Concerned educators throughout the district developed a plan for a newcomer school for high school students that included the following components: (1) an orientation to American culture and American school life through the native language or SDAIE (when teachers speaking the native language of students could not be found); (2) integration of ESOL and content classes in order to enhance both English and academic subject-matter development, and (3) content-area instruction in the native language, whenever possible, in order to maintain and further develop students' cognitive capabilities.

The district implemented the plan and made the school available to newcomers for up to 1 year. After that, students were transferred to their regular high schools. The newcomer school had a marked impact on the success rate of L2 students when they transferred to their home schools. Whereas, in the past, L2 students had struggled desperately and often dropped out, now they tended to stay in school and graduate.

Programming Myth #4: It is best for L2 students to be pulled out of their regular education classes for English language instruction.

Reality: It depends.

Background/Overview

Some districts hire specialist ESOL teachers, many of whom pull out students for specialized instruction. Teachers who are advocates of this model often comment that these opportunities to work with other students with similar needs place LEP students in a less stressful situation for at least some of the schoolday. That is, they are able to develop and express a degree of expertise that they are unlikely to encounter in the regular education class for several months, if not years.

Other ESOL teachers espouse a push-in model, in which they work in the regular classroom and collaborate closely with the classroom teacher (e.g., Syvanen 1993). In this way, ESOL teachers are able to address the particular needs of L2 students without having to remove them from the richness of the regular classroom environment. In some cases, ESOL teachers work exclusively with the ESOL students. In other cases, ESOL teachers work primarily with the L2 students, but often work with them in the context of small groups that include fluent and native English speakers. In yet other cases, the ESOL and regular education teachers are essentially co-teachers, and, although the ESOL teachers may be primarily responsible for teaching the L2 students, they also take responsibility for some whole-class teaching. The type of push-in model that teachers adopt is, to a large extent, influenced by the professional relationship that the teachers have and the knowledge base of the regular education teacher with regard to teaching L2 students. In a push-in model, it is essential that the collaborating teachers have sufficient time to plan together. As one might imagine, this model appears to be most successful when teachers choose to work together and when they share a common pedagogy.

Another factor to consider when planning the ESOL program is the degree to which L2 students are pulled out of their classrooms for special classes (e.g., migrant education, speech and language, Title I reading, ESOL). It is not unusual to encounter students who spend much more time outside their regular education classrooms than they do in their regular classes, and the reactions of teachers to this phenomenon vary. Some teachers despair that they never have time to get to know and help their L2 students, and wonder how the students can benefit from interactions with their peers if they are rarely around to develop friendships with other class members. Other teachers are relieved that someone else is dealing with the special needs of the L2 learners. What is most important, however, is the effect of this type of situation on the L2 students, linguistically, academically, and emotionally. Are the various classes for which the students are being pulled out integrated and collaboratively planned by the various teachers involved? If not, schools should seriously reconsider simply placing their L2 students in a fragmented program made up of several pull-out classes.

Scenario

In March, just before Spring Break, the sixth-grade teachers at Kennedy Middle School met at lunchtime to discuss their L2 students' progress. All of their students would have to take a state-mandated test in late April, and they wanted to be sure that their L2 students would be able to do well. In the course of the conversation, they realized that they barely knew their L2 students, particularly those who were newcomers to the United States. It turned out that, in a well-intended effort to provide as much support as possible, these students spent over half of the day outside their regular education classrooms. They spent two periods a day with the ESOL teacher, one period a day with the speech and language teacher, and one period a day with the reading specialist. When the teachers took into account that their newcomer L2 students were with their English-speaking peers only during mathematics and specials such as PE, music, and art (which were taught by other teachers), they realized that the program for L2 students really wasn't a program, but a fragmented hodgepodge of classes.

This absence of knowledge about their L2 students was further compounded by the fact that the classroom teachers had very little contact with the specialist teachers, other than through a weekly written communication in which the classroom teacher indicated what she or he would be focusing on the next week in the content classes, and specialist teachers briefly noted what they had focused on. All of the specialist teachers worked in more than one school, making it more difficult for the teachers to meet and coordinate all services to L2 students.

The sixth-grade teachers realized that this state of affairs needed to change. They arranged to meet with the principal, who was receptive to their concerns. He set up a meeting for the next week with all the teachers who worked with the L2 learners, and also raised the teachers' concerns with central office staff responsible for the different special programs. In the short term, the principal used staff development funds to compensate the teachers for meeting on a weekly basis to plan for and coordinate services to L2 learners; the principal attended most of these meetings, and when unable to attend, made sure that the teachers kept him fully informed.

One early outcome of these weekly meetings was that the ESOL teacher and one of the sixth-grade teachers began to implement a push-in model. Before implementing the model, they met with an ESOL teacher from another district who had several years experience in push-in ESOL teaching; his insights (and continuing support) helped the two teachers at Kennedy Middle School as they collaborated. By the end of the semester, they felt that it had been a successful collaboration, and they wanted to use the summer to reflect on what they had learned and to plan thoroughly for the following year. Despite their colleagues' enthusiasm, the other sixth-grade teachers chose not to participate in a push-in program for the following year.

When the Kennedy teachers alerted their principal to the fragmented nature of services to L2 students, it sparked a series of actions on the part of the district that led to much-improved services for all L2 students in the district. For example, the Director of Curriculum authorized summer curriculum development funds to pay a group of teachers and administrators to develop an integrated program for L2 students. Over the summer, this group of educators prepared a plan that identified students' needs; analyzed the effectiveness and appropriateness of existing programs and staffing plans; suggested assessment procedures and resources for identifying L2 students with special needs; recommended staffing (e.g., hiring additional ESOL teachers); and developed a list of suggested assessment and instructional strategies and resources for classroom teachers when working with L2 students. The

Director of Curriculum also arranged for two professors from a neighboring university who specialized in teaching L2 learners to assist in developing and implementing a staff development plan for the following year. Each school in the district identified two to three teachers who wished to become better prepared in teaching L2 students, and would act as local resources in their schools, along with the ESOL teachers. By the end of the next schoolyear, several classroom teachers had begun to work very closely with the ESOL teachers, who now had major responsibility for providing specialized services to L2 learners.

Programming Myth #5: It's against the law to segregate students, so we don't offer special classes for L2 learners— neither bilingual nor ESOL classes. We don't want to be out of compliance with the law.

Reality: In order to receive the most appropriate education, L2 students may need to be placed in specialized programs that serve only L2 learners.

Background/Overview

When discussing the education of L2 students, many educators become confused by what constitutes segregation. The segregation of African American students in the United States was intended to keep African American students separate from white students. It was not a carefully designed program to enhance the learning of African American students. In the case of L2 students, some of the program options for L2 learners separate these students for at least part of the school day from native English speakers (e.g., bilingual education, pull-out ESOL, SDAIE, and newcomer centers). In contrast with segregated education, these programs are designed not to keep students of different races apart, but to act as a temporary measure to ensure the academic achievement and English language development of L2 students.

It is interesting to note that some recent innovations in programming for L2 learners incorporate more contact with native English speakers. Two-way immersion programs and push-in ESOL programs are two examples. In the case of two-way immersion programs, L2 students who speak the same native language are placed with students who are fluent speakers of English. Both groups of students learn language and content through two languages—English and the other language. These programs are predicated on the understanding that naturally occurring and meaningful interactions with native speakers of the target languages will enhance the language development of both groups of students. Also, these programs are thought to enhance cross-cultural understanding, something that is often missing in interactions involving minority and majority language students. In other cases, teachers collaborate with regular education teachers in offering their students a cross-age tutoring experience (Cook & Urzúa 1993; Hoffman & Heath 1986; Samway, Whang & Pippitt 1995). In many cases, this cross-age experience provides L2 students with opportunities to use English in a meaningful, stress-free way.

Scenario

A suburban school district, Woodland Heights, has become home to increasing numbers of L2 students as a consequence of the opening of a software factory in the vicinity. In the past, the district had virtually no L2 students. The district now has approximately ninety L2 students in grades K–5, in two of the three elementary schools. At one of the monthly meetings of district administrators, they discuss what they can and should do with their L2 students. They had earlier decided that it would be best to place the L2 students with teachers who were more nurturing, which had become the guiding principle in placement decisions. Some of these teachers had begun to question why they were always selected when a new L2 student entered the school. While it was true that they were noticeably effective at connecting with students, it had been very discouraging for them to realize that they couldn't understand or talk with these students, let alone connect with them. They began to wonder what was wrong with the students— Why weren't they speaking English after 3 months in the class? Why didn't they play with the English-speaking children at recess? Did they even want to learn English?

The teachers were confused, discouraged, and angry. Some of them talked with friends in other districts and discovered that many of these districts had special programs for their L2 learners. Some districts had bilingual programs. Other districts had hired ESOL teachers, who worked with groups of L2 learners on a daily basis. One district had established a modified self-contained newcomer program, where L2 students spent the entire day with other L2 learners while they learned English and the content-area subjects through the native language or English. Armed with this information, the teachers approached their principals . . . which led to the discussion at the monthly meeting of district administrators mentioned earlier. At this meeting, the Assistant Superintendent commented that the district had very good teachers, perhaps the best in the region, and they should be able to teach the newcomer students. Perhaps the district could offer some workshops to the teachers? He reminded the other administrators that it was illegal to segregate students, and he was concerned not to be out of compliance during the upcoming state review.

During the state review of the district, staff members from the ESL/Bilingual Office visited classes and interviewed teachers, administrators, and students. They discovered that the L2 students did not receive any special services, other than a half hour twice a week with a volunteer who was a student at a local college—she hoped to enter the teaching credential program and this volunteer work would fulfill the program's preprofessional experience requirement. It became very clear to the reviewers that the L2 students were in a "sink or swim"/submersion situation, because the teachers were not knowledgeable about second language acquisition or L2 teaching approaches and techniques. The review team cited the district for inappropriately and inadequately serving L2 students. In the exit interview, they explained how segregating students because of race or ethnicity was illegal, but providing students with bilingual and ESOL programs to ensure the students' academic and linguistic success was not illegal.

Programming Myth #6: LEP students are precluded from participating in Title I services and programs.

Reality: LEP services can receive Title I services and participate in Title I programs.

Background/Overview

Many educators have long held the belief that Title I was not available to serve LEP students (Hakuta & August 1993). Title I has *always* been available to help meet the needs of LEP students (particularly in academic areas —even in the first language of the students), but could not be applied to providing such students with specialized ESOL instruction (which is the responsibility of the local school district).

With the advent of the Improving America's Schools Act (IASA), the reauthorization of the Elementary and Secondary Education Act, and the growth of Title I schoolwide programs, a school's ability to serve its L2 students is greatly enhanced (August et al. 1995). Schoolwide programs are those that target the entire school (rather than just a particular population of students) and are designed to serve schools with high-poverty student populations (usually defined as 50% or more of the total school population).

Schoolwide programs serving large concentrations of LEP students and language minority students can be tailored to meet the specific academic and cultural needs of the children by providing schoolwide catch-up help in academic areas for students whose education in their native language has been delayed or interrupted, by providing "sheltered content" classes (i.e., academic classes in subjects such as math or science, taught through specialized techniques that reduce the linguistic load) or specialized programs that help language minority students meet new, higher academic standards.

Chapter 8

Staffing and Staff
Development Myths

Staffing/Staff Development Myth #1: ESOL teachers
must be able to speak a language other than English.

Reality: To be an ESOL teacher, it is not necessary (though
it can be very helpful) to speak a language other than English
because the language of instruction is English.

Background/Overview

Knowledge of another language is not usually a requirement to be an ESOL teacher, although some states require that teachers be familiar with a nonnative language. For example, in California, all candidates for the Crosscultural, Language, and Academic
Development (CLAD) emphasis credential or certificate (which certifies them to teach L2
students in English) must have experiecne learning a second language. The intention is to
sensitize teachers to the experience of learning a nonnative language, rather than to prepare
teachers to communicate with students in their native languages, as is the case with bilingual teachers. Many ESOL teachers are, in fact, speakers of more than one language. However, there are many very effective ESOL teachers who are monolingual English speakers.

In many countries, English is taught to children from a very early age, and as a result, adults are often very fluent speakers of English, albeit with a nonnative accent. Some
of them become teachers, and when they immigrate to the United States, they often pursue their U.S. teaching credentials. In some districts, there is the belief that an ESOL
teacher must be a native speaker of English. There are many very well prepared, experienced, successful ESOL teachers who are not native speakers of English. Although command of English is a very important factor to consider when hiring teaching personnel,
it is wise to also consider other factors, including previous experience, professional preparation, knowledge of current pedagogy, and sensitivity to the experiences of L2 students.

Scenario

*Before the school year begins for students, the faculty and staff at West Side School Dis-
trict gather together for a districtwide orientation to the year. At the end of this half-day*

meeting, the Associate Superintendent for Curriculum and Instruction announces that Magda Stanovich, an ESOL teacher at P.S. 42, has been named outstanding teacher by the district selection panel. She received the award for her commitment to and advocacy on behalf of newcomer students, excellence in teaching, and commitment to enhancing the profession through her mentoring work of new teachers. The teachers and principal from Magda's school, as well as other ESOL teachers who have worked closely with Magda, stand and cheer as Magda goes up to receive her award. Half an hour later, during lunch, a group of teachers is talking about Magda's winning this coveted award:

Betty: How on earth could she get that award? She doesn't even speak English right.

Rhoda: Yeah. Have you heard her accent? And to think she teaches English. What nerve.

Delia: What do you mean? So she's got a bit of an accent, but she's a tremendous teacher. I used to work right next to her and she was really good. I never saw kids so motivated and excited about learning as I saw in her class. Yeah, she's got an accent, but have you noticed that she speaks excellent English? I bet her vocabulary and grammar are better than ours!

Rhoda: But ESOL kids need fluent speaker models.

Delia: What they need is someone who knows how to teach them English and understands what they're going through. And she understands that. Anyway, she is fluent. It's not like her accent gets in the way of understanding. You can understand her OK, can't you? (Betty and Rhoda do not say anything) What if she had a French accent? I bet you'd say she had a lovely accent! An Eastern European accent isn't quite so attractive is it?! (She laughs) No, I think we need more teachers like Magda. She knows what she's doing, and she puts the kids ahead of everything. You know, I was really surprised that she got the award because she speaks up when she sees things aren't right. She's made a few enemies along the way. I thought it was great to see her get the award.

Staffing/Staff Development Myth #2: When hiring bilingual teachers, districts can assume that teachers who possess a bilingual credential are fluent in a language other than English.

Reality: There are some teachers who have a bilingual credential, but are not fluent in the target language.

Background/Overview

There is a tremendous shortage of bilingual teachers across the nation, not just in the states with the greatest number of L2 students. (Macías [1989] estimated that between 68,000 and 100,000 were needed, but these figures are almost a decade old and the LEP population has grown exponentially since that time.) As a consequence, it is not uncommon to find districts hiring teachers who are not actually bilingual and biliterate. The most common problems that we have encountered include the following:

1. Some teachers with bilingual teaching credentials are not orally fluent in the non-English language (e.g., Spanish or Vietnamese) and/or are not fluent readers and writers of the language. It is therefore wise when hiring bilingual teachers, to ask a fluent speaker/writer of the non-English language to assess candidates' ability to communicate and teach through this language.

2. Because of the shortage of bilingual teachers, many districts invite non-bilingual teachers to work towards a bilingual teaching certificate, assign them to bilingual classes, and pay them extra for their efforts. Although some of these teachers become fluent speakers of a language other than English and prove to be excellent bilingual teachers, there are others who do not make much progress in the target language, never become bilingual, and move to a non-bilingual teaching position once the allocated time for earning the bilingual credential (e.g., 3–7 years) runs out.

3. In some districts, personnel see a bilingual teaching certificate and neglect to check which languages the teacher speaks. Certified bilingual teachers are then placed in a bilingual classroom, but not one that is taught in their languages of expertise (e.g., a Japanese-English-speaking teacher being placed in a Russian-English bilingual class). We do not mean to belabor the point, but it is crucial to place bilingual teachers with students who speak the language for which the teachers are certified.

4. Native speakers of the target language, who are teachers in their native lands, are hired as bilingual teachers. On occasion, these teachers are not fluent speakers of English. Some districts have addressed this dilemma by pairing a teacher who is a fluent English speaker with a teacher who is a fluent speaker of another language. These two teachers teach in their dominant languages, share two classes, and exchange classes either each day, every other day, or every week.

Scenario

In a large city school district, there are many L2 students, and the district is under a court order to provide bilingual instruction for students who attend schools with large concentrations of Spanish, Vietnamese, Laotian, and Chinese. The district hires Joan Armstrong-Estrada, a Spanish-English teacher, to teach a Spanish-English bilingual kindergarten class. After 2 years, she is inexplicably switched to a Laotian-English bilingual class, where she is assisted by a Laotian-speaking instructional aide. The district hires a non-Spanish-speaking teacher to take over the Spanish-English bilingual kindergarten. When Joan voices her concerns to her principal, she is told that it's out of his hands and that they want her there because she's a good teacher and the class needs a good teacher. It takes her an entire year of petitioning to get reassigned to the Spanish-English bilingual kindergarten classroom.

Staffing/Staff Development Myth #3: We don't have that many L2 learners, so we don't need to hire ESOL or bilingual teachers.

Reality: The number of L2 students in U.S. schools continues to grow, and, because settlement patterns of immigrant families are not predictable, it is wise for districts to plan for a future that includes L2 students. Hence, when hiring teachers and other staff, it is advisable to hire those with ESOL or bilingual certification and/or experience.

Background/Overview

Some districts have a long history of working with L2 students and have used the intervening years to hire the best-qualified staff. In other cases, districts are relative newcomers to working with L2 students (or have not made this population a priority until now) and need to begin from scratch. It is important to anticipate future needs when considering staffing (e.g., number of LEP students, any changes in languages spoken by students entering the district, changes in the age of entering students), in addition to current trends (*Staffing the Multilingual Impacted Schools of the 1990's*, 1990).

When working on staffing, it is critical to assess the need for knowledgeable and culturally sensitive employees in a variety of roles, including teachers, administrators, interpreters, instructional aides, counselors, community liaisons-outreach workers, playground supervisors, and librarians (Lucas, Henze & Donato 1990). Many districts have effectively established career ladders that enable them to successfully tap into the language resources of the community. Through these programs, community members who are, for example, bilingual instructional aides, receive support that allows them to become teachers. Community members are nurtured through the system, often with considerable support from local colleges and universities. It is also very helpful to hire content-area faculty who are knowledgeable about both the subject matter and second language acquisition theory and practice (Cantoni-Harvey 1987; Rivera & Vehler 1990).

Scenario

Four years ago, when Lincoln School District revisited its long-term plan, it realized that it needed to plan for the much larger numbers of L2 students that it currently had in the district. This was grounded in the experiences of neighboring districts, which had experienced a marked increase in the enrollment of L2 students once a small but labor-intensive industrial park on the outskirts of town began to be constructed. Although the district addressed all grades in their long-term planning, it paid particular attention to the secondary grades because it knew that many of the newcomer students in the neighboring districts were undereducated refugees from Southeast Asia and Central America.

The teaching force in the district was very experienced, but each year many teachers retired. When finding replacements for these teachers, the district made a concerted effort to ensure that all new teachers to the district had an ESOL teaching certificate and/ or were bilingual in Spanish, Laotian, or Vietnamese; those with experience working with L2 students were preferred. When hiring other personnel (e.g., administrators, counselors, playground staff), the district also looked for people with background experiences and expertise working with L2 populations. The district advertised extensively, through ESOL, bilingual, and subject-matter professional organizations and publications; through employment displays at regional, state, and national conferences; and through contacts to teacher-preparation programs.

The district realized that it needed to plan for content-area instruction for secondary LEP students by identifying teachers who were interested in becoming ESOL specialists as well. These teachers then received intensive preparation in second language acquisition and SDAIE. In this way, the district ensured that they would have on staff teachers who were knowledgeable about both the subject matter and second language acquisition theory and practice. These teachers had opportunities to implement what they were learning about teaching L2 students because they had one or two such students in some of their classes.

The district's hunch proved right, as, about 2 years ago, the district registered over 100 newcomer high school students in less than 2 weeks. The content-area teachers who had received SDAIE preparation were reassigned for three to four periods a day to teach newcomer L2 students. Fortunately, because of advanced planning and preparation, the high school was able to handle the influx of students quite well—not without a struggle, but without the chaos that frequently accompanies a sudden influx of students with specialized needs.

Staffing/Staff Development Myth #4: Staff development money and resources relating to the education of L2 students should be directed to the teachers, because they are the people responsible for teaching them.

Reality: Staff development should target all personnel.

Background/Overview

When planning staff development, it is wise to consider the needs of employees with different responsibilities (e.g., teachers, administrators, instructional assistants, clerical staff, home/school liaisons). In fact, anyone who comes in contact with L2 students and/or their families should be provided with appropriate, focused staff development. Research indicates that programs that are comprehensive and include all staff (not just teachers) contribute a great deal to successful programs for LEP students (see Lucas, Henze & Donato 1990; McKeon & Malarz 1991; Tikunoff et al. 1991).

Scenario

Del Vista High School, located in a rural area that is rapidly becoming a suburb, has seen an increase in racially motivated incidents. For example, Vietnamese and Latino students have been taunted and jumped at bus stops, anti-immigrant graffiti has appeared on school walls, and one member of the janitorial staff refused to clean the ESOL classroom, saying "I'm not cleaning up after illegal aliens who take jobs away from Americans." At first, the principal tried to contain the incidents by having the graffiti painted over, suspending two students for instigating fights, and arranging for the janitor to be transferred to another school in the district. It was only after the local newspaper reported on the incidents that the principal and other administrators realized that they had a serious situation on their hands.

At the urging of two teachers who were active in a local social justice organization, the principal contacted a regional desegregation center. A team of staff members from this center made a 2-day visit to the school and interviewed groups of students, teachers, clerical staff, administrators, counselors, and janitors. This visit led to a year-long, multifaceted attempt to reverse the cross-cultural ignorance and animosity that was pervasive in the school. The plan was developed by a planning group that included students, faculty, staff, and one of the desegregation center staff members who had previous experience working with high schools. The plan that was implemented that year included the following:

1. *A series of workshops for all faculty and staff, which focused on the legal rights of immigrants and refugees and information about the language, culture, and contributions of minority groups in the United States, particularly those groups represented in the school, were set up. All faculty and staff had to attend a series of workshops, but they had choice over which series to attend.*

2. *A conflict-resolution program for students that used peer conflict managers was implemented.*

3. *The social studies and English departments revised their core curricula and related readings and materials so that they reflected a much more diverse world than had been the case earlier.*

4. *A PTSA-funded Artists-in-the-Schools program was implemented—a multicultural street theater group put on interactive shows about cross-cultural issues, followed by small group discussions.*

Although these actions did not eradicate racial and ethnic biases and tensions, there was a marked increase in cross-cultural understanding and tolerance.

Staffing/Staff Development Myth #5: When considering staffing needs with regard to the L2 student population, we need to concentrate on classroom teachers.

Reality: When hiring, evaluating performance, and planning for staff development, it is important to consider the expertise of all staff members, not just teachers.

Background/Overview

Even a well-designed, thoughtful, and visionary plan for a district or school will probably fail if the appropriate staff are not hired to implement what has been planned. Although teachers are at the heart of schools, care should also be taken to assess how well other staff members mesh with the program goals. This means that when hiring, evaluating, and planning staff development activities, the expertise, cultural sensitivity, and needs of all faculty and staff are to be considered (i.e., for teachers, administrators, interpreters, instructional aides, clerical and service workers, counselors, psychologists, playground supervisors, librarians, community outreach workers, etc.).

Many schools experience problems when counselors and community outreach personnel do not speak the native language or know anything about the home cultures of L2 students. Although translators and community resources can often help in such situations, having fluent speakers of target languages on staff can be very beneficial. Similarly, a librarian who lacks knowledge about or interest in multicultural fiction and nonfiction or literature written in languages other than English is less likely to be as successful at working with L2 students as will a librarian who has made a point of becoming knowledgeable about these books.

Scenario

In collaboration with a local university, Baker Unified School District, a mid-sized, urban K through 8 school district, established a K through 5 professional development school (PDS). The district had experienced expanding enrollment and needed to build a new school, so took this opportunity to develop a center where the district's teachers could receive ongoing staff development and preservice teachers could work with experienced expert teachers. Because many of the lowest-achieving students in the district were native Spanish speakers from low-income homes, the district decided to place a heavy emphasis on this population in the PDS. When the school opened, grades K through 2 had two-way Spanish immersion classes. Each year, a grade was added, so that at the end of 3 years, the school had a two-way Spanish immersion class at each grade. The district debated long and hard about whether they wanted the school to be only a two-way immersion program, and decided that they should offer classes at each grade level that were regular education classes taught in English.

A year before the school was built, during the summer, the district identified the principal for this school, Ana Morales, an experienced administrator who had been principal at another school in the district, where she had been very effective and was highly regarded by faculty, staff, and community members. The district advertised the positions that would be available at the school, and, during the first part of the fall semester, they identified faculty and staff for the school. All of the faculty and resource personnel (e.g., resource reading teacher, ESOL teacher, speech and language teacher, instructional aides) were either Spanish–English bilingual teachers or were experienced teachers of ESOL students; many had a master's degree in TESOL or Bilingual Education.

The district knew that students' success in school would also be affected by non-teaching personnel, such as the home/school coordinator, the school secretary, and the lunchroom staff. All of these staff members were bilingual and were involved with all planning and staff development. A core group of parents and community members also joined the planning group.

*Although Ana Morales was released to coordinate the planning for and develop-
ment of the PDS before the school opened, the other faculty and staff remained in their
current placements until the school was ready to open, but were released for regular
planning meetings. For the remainder of the year, this team collaborated in (1) assisting
the architect and contractor in designing the school, (2) developing a vision for the
school, (3) planning programs and identifying necessary resources and materials, and
(4) meeting with family and community members to talk with them about the new
school and to register students for the school.*

Staffing/Staff Development Myth #6: There's no way we can provide intensive staff development on issues relating to L2 students—we don't have the resources.

Reality: When districts allocate sufficient resources to intensive, ongoing, substantive staff development on issues relating to L2 students, their efforts are usually realized in the greater academic achievement of L2 students.

Background/Overview

The challenge of educating LEP students brings with it special needs for staff development. When there is a crisis, as schools frequently experience when there is a sudden influx of LEP students, there is often a tendency to address the issue quickly with
a workshop. These kinds of staff development designs are often comparable to applying a Band-Aid to a deep cut, and they rarely lead to substantive or long-term
change. It is important to draw upon the broad body of literature on effective staff
development practices when designing programs that focus on working with LEP
students. Some principles to consider include the following:

1. If faculty and staff are involved in the development of an inservice plan (e.g.,
   content, design, frequency and type of inservice), it is more likely that their
   needs will be met and they will be more invested in the process and content than
   if they had not been involved.

2. Although it may be very tempting, when one sees a glaring need, to mandate attendance at a particular staff development event, it is generally much more effective to offer choices to participants. While it is reasonable to require that all
   faculty and staff become knowledgeable about a critical area or issue that the
   school or district is confronting, it is generally wiser to offer choices. Unless the
   faculty is unanimous in the topic to be explored, it is worth offering alternatives.
   Experience has taught us that to do otherwise is to treat the ongoing development of faculty and staff in a short-sighted way.

3. It is not usually a good idea to rely on "shot-in-the-dark" staff development experiences. Workshops and conferences can be very stimulating and can provide
   for short-term bursts of learning. However, without longer-term opportunities
   to absorb, reflect on, and act on what one is learning, the impact on faculty and

staff (and students' learning) is likely to be limited. It is best, therefore, to organize staff development over time, perhaps over the course of a whole year, thereby giving participants opportunities to share experiences in follow-up sessions. Sometimes it is advisable to coordinate plans with other schools in the district or neighboring districts that have similar needs. In this way, specialized needs of faculty and staff may be better addressed.

4. Staff development that focuses on LEP students should ensure that the content takes into account both linguistic features of language acquisition and the sociocultural context in which language is learned and used. In the past, considerable attention was paid to grammatical structures and vocabulary. However, successful language learning and acquisition is grounded in knowledge about how language is used in particular contexts, for example, differences in how one would greet close friends ("Hey, man!" or "Yo!") and adult strangers (e.g., "Hello" or "Good morning"). In addition, educators need to pay attention to the degree to which students have opportunities to use language in natural settings within the classroom (e.g., to negotiate meaning with a small group of peers, to explain a choice, or to request information or help). In many schools, most of the talking is done by teachers and silent classrooms are highly valued. Neither situation is as helpful for language development as those classrooms in which students are responsible for a great deal of the talk.

We have noticed that, in some districts, a tremendous amount of money is dedicated to summer curriculum development work, much of which ends up sitting on shelves, not achieving the wider goals that were anticipated. Teachers who have participated in, for example, the design of thematic units may benefit a great deal from this work, but other teachers may not derive much benefit from their products, because they have not been involved in the process of developing the materials. Also, the needs, interests, and abilities of classes vary from classroom to classroom and from year to year. In addition, placing so much focus on unit activities inevitably places much more focus on the activities and much less focus on the learners.

Scenario

At Loma Linda School, a Spanish-English bilingual K through 6 magnet school, the faculty and staff decided that one of their program goals would be to develop the writing fluency of students in both Spanish and English. The school already placed emphasis on writing; for example, each classroom had a daily writers' workshop, during which students wrote on self-selected topics and conferred with their peers, and teachers taught writing skills and strategies as needed, to the whole class, small groups, and individual students. However, the teachers weren't sure whether students were actually improving as writers; in addition, they didn't really know the extent to which students were writing in both languages. In collaboration with the district evaluator, they decided to assess this goal (to develop the writing fluency of students in both languages) in a variety of ways:

1. On a monthly basis, each teacher reviewed all writing folders and tallied which pieces were written in the native language or English. This monthly log indicated over time the extent to which students were writing in Spanish and English.

2. On a monthly basis, teachers and students independently selected the best piece of writing for that month, provided a brief description of why they considered it best, and placed it in the student's long-term writing folder. At mid-year and at the end of the year, a randomly selected group of students' writing from each class was assessed holistically to determine whether writing had improved over time.

3. During writers' workshop, teachers began to systematically write brief notes on individual students' writing processes and development: For example, "Juanita wrote for the first time today in English. She said she needed to use English because she was writing to last year's teacher, who didn't know Spanish. She demonstrated awareness of the needs of her audience." These were dated and placed in a folder or notebook in which each page was devoted to an individual student. To ensure that no students would be overlooked, the teachers devised a plan whereby each student was observed at least once per week. These observations provided contextualized data that helped the teachers record significant developments.

Work sessions conducted during the first half of the year helped the faculty explore features of successful writing (e.g., cohesiveness, clarity of topic development, effective use of illustrations, effective use of detail, presence of writers' voices), and these became guidelines for the holistic scoring descriptors for each grade level. They also helped the teachers make instructional decisions. Twice a year (mid-year and at the end of the year) the teachers met together for holistic scoring sessions. At this time, they randomly sampled half of the folders in each class and assessed each piece of writing in the folders. The writing of both Spanish-dominant and English-dominant students was represented in the selection of folders. The teachers then compared the scores to establish whether writing had improved over time; pieces written in Spanish were compared with each other and pieces written in English were compared with each other.

After only 1 month, the faculty was able to see that students wrote in English an overwhelming percentage of the time, even when they were not able to write more than an isolated word or two. This observation concerned the teachers, because they believed strongly in the transferability of writing processes from one language to the other and realized that the least fluent students would probably develop their writing more successfully if they were to write in Spanish, at least initially. This observation also caused the teachers to reflect on possible causes. After monitoring their own roles during writers' workshop, they realized that they usually talked with students in English, and when they shared their own writing with students, which they did to varying degrees of frequency, it was usually written in English. They wondered if they had inadvertently been stressing that writing in English was the desired outcome. The teachers decided that if they were to enhance the writing development of their students, particularly those who were most limited in English, they would need to model writing in Spanish, which they embarked on immediately. In the months that followed, the teachers made an effort to balance the degree to which they used and wrote in Spanish and English, placing more focus on Spanish. By the end of the year students were writing more in Spanish, but they also continued to write in English.

*The holistic scoring confirmed that, in most cases, students had become more flu-
ent writers over the course of the school year, which was important information to include
in the school report to the district and for the district to report to the state and federal
funding sources. At the mid-year holistic scoring session, it became apparent that several
students were abandoning many pieces of writing before they had been completed, which
resulted in many marginally developed pieces. Through discussions with each other, the
evaluator, and the students, the teachers realized that the students often regarded the writing in writers' workshop as an exercise, rather than a genuine effort to communicate with
others. The students enjoyed writing their drafts, but they had not had many opportunities to truly experience what is involved in writing for an audience other than oneself, as
most of the writing stayed in the folders, instead of being taken to publication (e.g., for a
class or school newsletter, for submission to a nationally published student magazine, for
publication as a book, which would then be placed in the school or classroom library). The
teachers began to focus more on purposes for writing, different audiences and their needs,
and when and how to publish. The faculty and staff also decided to start their own writing group; they began to experience first-hand what is involved in writing for others and
were able to share their insights, processes, and experiences with students, which seemed
to have a positive effect on what students were willing to do as writers.*

*Holistic scoring was helpful in providing data on the extent to which writing had
improved over time. However, the faculty discovered that it did not provide the kind of in-
depth analysis of individual students' writing development and processes that they wished
to pass on to subsequent teachers. This is where the anecdotal records and cumulative writing folders with comments on why pieces were included were helpful. When teachers met
with parents and caregivers, they were able to draw upon these various sources of data. The
data were also helpful to the evaluator, who, when writing reports, supplemented data on
which language was used when writing with a narrative description and discussion of what
the students had accomplished and future directions to explore.*

Staffing/Staff Development Myth #7: We need to fo-
cus our planning on the immediate situation posed by our
L2 students; we can deal with long-term planning later.

Reality: It is advisable to focus on both short-term and
long-term goals and plans.

Background/Overview

In the turmoil that often accompanies crisis situations in schools, it is easy to neglect
to take a step back and thoughtfully and collaboratively develop a vision and long-
term goals for a program. Although it is true that a crisis situation requires immediate attention, it is generally very useful to use this experience as the springboard for
long-term planning.

Effective program planning invariably relies on a well-thought-through vision
for the school on the part of faculty, staff, students, and community members. The
development of a vision can help a school or district clearly delineate the goals it has

for LEP students, while also ensuring that these goals are comparable to those held for non-LEP students. While this observation has common sense validity, it is supported by research (e.g., Lucas, Henze & Donato 1990). Districts that have addressed the challenge of educating LEP students most successfully often have a clear vision for their program. Instead of opting to comply with minimal requirements as quickly and easily as possible and leaving it at that, they address the immediate need, but also take time to carefully establish what they think an excellent and effective program would look like. It is often a good idea to establish two visions, one that is short term (e.g., in situations in which there is a sudden and unexpected change in either the number of LEP students or the native languages spoken) and one that is long-term (e.g., a 3- to 5-year strategic plan). It is unlikely that the number of LEP students will suddenly drop, so it is important not to be caught off guard.

Scenario

A large, inner-city elementary school district, Evergreen, recently announced that each school would have 4 months in which to develop a plan for educating nonnative English speakers because they were not achieving on a par with other students in the district. Because the district has gradually become home to large numbers of immigrants and refugees from Asia, Southeast Asia, and Latin America, administrators recognize the need for all teachers to have some expertise in teaching nonnative speakers. It has hired Spanish-English bilingual teachers to work in two schools that have large numbers of elementary-aged Spanish-speaking students, and it now hires only teachers who have the state supplementary ESOL or bilingual credential.

Although the district is dedicated to hiring new faculty and staff who are appropriately certified and knowledgeable about working with L2 learners, it has not done much to address the limitations of other, more established teachers. One avenue that it has introduced is to pay for teachers to attend a 30-hour series of workshops offered by the county office of education. However, these workshops have minimal impact on upgrading the teachers' skills because the workshops are designed to help teachers pass the state test that leads to the supplementary ESOL credential. Although the teachers often pass the test, they are very honest about how little they still know about teaching L2 students because the workshops are so geared to the test, rather than the needs of the teachers. Taking the workshops helps the district comply with state regulations regarding the paper credentials of teachers who work with LEP students, but it does not improve teaching or student achievement.

The district mandate for program development generated significant discussion at Hope Elementary School, a multitrack, year-round school with large numbers of LEP students who speak twenty-two distinct languages. The teachers and principal realized that they needed to talk about what their goals were for all students, particularly LEP students, and the rationale for these goals. They believed that developing an educational plan would help them in several ways: (1) better conceptualize the instructional direction for their school; (2) identify what they knew about language and literacy development and teaching, and what they needed to know more about; and (3) decide how staff development funds could best be spent to help them achieve their goals.

The faculty met on several occasions within the 4 months available to them to develop their plan, but they continued meeting throughout the year to further refine it. After a few meetings, they realized that they needed to be working with all members of the staff at the school, not just the teachers and principal, so office staff and instructional aides became part of the planning group. Throughout the process, they read widely, talked with experts, attended conferences, visited other schools, and talked among themselves as they developed and rethought their plan. The faculty and staff eventually came to consensus on their goals, which included the following: (1) bring LEP students on a par with native English-speaking peers, (2) enhance students' native language and literacy, (3) integrate students' experiences and cultures into learning experiences, and (4) assess students on an ongoing basis.

The faculty decided to begin with the first goal (bring LEP students on a par with native English-speaking peers), as they felt that it was all-encompassing and would allow them to address all goals, at least some of the time. This goal was of particular concern to them because many LEP students enter the school in the intermediate grades and always struggled to catch up with their native English-speaking peers who had already received content instruction in English for several years. The faculty recognized that L2 students often need several years in which to become fluent in English and academically successful. However, they decided to set this high goal so as to challenge themselves to institute programs and approaches that would enhance the language, literacy, and content learning of the most needy students. They had seen how, in past years, the LEP students had often been left to acquire English as best they could and with little direct support from the teachers, who were often terrified of this responsibility. They realized that they needed to provide all students with challenging content, while taking into account students' relative fluency in English. To accomplish this, many of the teachers acknowledged that they needed to radically alter their teaching styles by for example, exploring more hands-on, collaborative, inquiry-based, and integrated models of teaching that allow learners to construct meaning.

Chapter 9

Involving Parents and
the Community

Parent and Community Myth #1: We've tried to get
our parents involved, but they don't seem to care about
how well their children are doing in school; if they did,
they'd answer our phone calls and come to parent-teacher
conferences.

Reality: There are often good reasons why L2 parents
don't come to school, and we need to pursue alternative
ways of involving parents and working collaboratively
with them.

Background/Overview

For several years now, there has been increased awareness of the correlation between
the academic achievement of children and the degree to which parents are known to
be involved with their children's schooling. A large proportion of underachieving
students come from minority backgrounds, many from nonnative English-speaking
homes, which further compounds the problem because teachers rarely understand
the cultural or linguistic backgrounds of families, making for limited communica-
tions. It is essential that educators become knowledgeable about the communities
from which students come so that they may have more success as teachers and so that
students have more success as learners (Moll 1992; Simich-Dudgeon 1986; Violand-
Sanchez, Sutton & Ware 1991).

Traditionally, parent involvement has meant parents and other family members coming to school for open houses and conferences. Particularly in low-income
schools and secondary schools, parental attendance is often rather low, causing
teachers to complain that parents don't care about their children's success in school.
The opposite is generally true (e.g., Chavkin 1989), and schools need to explore
mechanisms that ensure that parents are informed and involved in the academic lives
of their children. Schools also need to take into account the needs of the community,
including their wishes for the children.

There are many ways in which school personnel and parents-community members can work together cooperatively. Menacker, Hurwitz, and Weldon (1988) discuss four levels of cooperation:

1. *Parents as clients:* Parents are informed about "good news," for example, through newsletters, telephone calls, notes, and home visits. Teachers are rewarded for their efforts through school rituals and inexpensive tokens of appreciation.

2. *Parents as producers:* Parents do tasks that are valued and appreciated by teachers, for example, playground supervision, clerical work, classroom assistance, security patrols. Jobs may be volunteer or paid, and financial resources may be required for parent orientation, training, salaries, and child care.

3. *Parents as consumers:* This involves a district-level commitment to offering evening and weekend programs for parents and community members. School faculty and staff should be used as instructors as much as possible so that parents and school personnel have opportunities to get to know each other. Potential participants need to be surveyed in order to offer programs that reflect parent–community interests and needs. Resources are needed to cover instructor salaries and child care for participants.

4. *Parents as governors:* Parents and community members are involved with shared decision making, for example, on developing policies for grading, homework, and discipline. Resources may be needed to ensure that parents and community members are well informed as they embark on this governance role.

Even when these four levels of cooperation are found in schools, parents and caregivers of LEP students are often marginalized if there is not attention paid to the need for translators and information printed in languages other than English.

These four categories of parent involvement neglect a role that parents and community members can frequently assume, that of expert. As educators, we often assume that we are the sole owners of knowledge and must act as conduits for the exchange of knowledge. It must be remembered that families and communities are also repositories of a great deal of shared knowledge, and it is worthwhile to tap into these sources of knowledge (Moll 1992).

Scenario

The principal at Lakeside School made it a priority to get to know the community, finding out who had special areas of expertise that the school could tap into. He quickly discovered that a local neighbor was an accomplished gardener, another was viewed as the expert on local history, another was a highly respected storyteller, another had been a professional baseball player, another was an expert baker, another did beautiful traditional bead work, another led a gospel choir. As the months passed, the list grew.

Friday afternoons at the school were devoted to special studies, which were led by teachers and had originally focused on the special interests of teachers (e.g., Chinese cooking, baseball card collecting, pastel drawing, drumming, volleyball, poetry writing). Students from across the grades selected a topic that lasted for 6 weeks; at the end of the

6 weeks, students made a new selection. In time, these special studies were led by com-
munity members, sometimes in collaboration with a teacher. Whenever necessary, the
principal made sure that translators were available, because the school community was
multilingual.

Community members also became resources for class-based projects and studies;
in fact, the special talents of family members and other community members began to
influence the selection and content of thematic studies. In addition, parents and com-
munity members became highly valued informants about special features of the lan-
guage and culture that had been causing misunderstandings; some community members
also acted as transmitters of the school culture and customs so that other members of the
community began to understand that when, for example, a teacher folded her arms, she
was not necessarily displaying antagonistic or hostile behavior towards the family mem-
bers. That is, all members of this complex school community began to understand each
other better than ever before, and the success of the approach was reflected in quite dra-
matic improvement in the academic success of students and in attendance rates.

Parent and Community Myth #2: It's impossible for us to involve L2 parents more, as most of our teachers are monolingual English speakers.

Reality: By taking small steps, schools can demonstrate to parents and community members that they are important and valued members of the school community that is educating their children.

Background/Overview

Although it can be quite daunting to consider ways of involving parents who may not
speak a lot of English, many schools and teachers have accomplished this very effectively. Some schools hold evening meetings on topics of interest to parents and arrange for translators who co-lead small group discussions with a monolingual
teacher, in addition to translating. Some schools turn parent-teacher conferences
into family mini-workshops, which the children lead. Some schools are very effective at tapping into community volunteers who are willing to act as translators, both
in conferences and in translating classroom and school letters and newsletters. Some
schools have implemented family literacy programs, which enhance family members'
English fluency, while also involving them in their children's education. Some
schools have worked hard to uncover the special skills and talents of community
members and nave then used them as resources.

Scenario

The first-grade teachers at Spring Valley Elementary School found the traditional twice-
yearly parent conferences to be rather exhausting and not particularly successful. They

were especially concerned that parents of newcomer students, mostly Chinese speakers, rarely came to these conferences. They were aware that attendance by Chinese-speaking parents was much higher in Barbara Chang and Faith Wong's second- and third-grade classrooms, respectively, which they attributed to these teachers being able to speak Chinese. Unable to speak Chinese, the first-grade teachers searched for an alternative strategy.

After talking with colleagues in a neighboring district who had very successfully implemented interactive parent-teacher conferences, they wondered if this would provide them with an answer to their dilemma. In these conferences, small groups of parents and their children visited the classroom for an hour. While the teacher conferred with each of the parent-child pairs or triads for 15 to 20 minutes, the rest of the children introduced their parents to what they were learning by working with them in five learning stations (language-literacy, mathematics, science, social studies, and interpersonal skills). At these stations, the children explained what they did (e.g., journal writing, poetry reading, sorting junk, interpreting graphs), and parents participated and asked questions (e.g., "How do you solve problems with other children in your classroom?" and "Tell me three scientific facts about the classroom pet, a snake.").

The teachers encouraged the language minority children to speak in their native languages with their parents. They also spent part of several days practicing how they would introduce their parents to their classroom and learning experiences. In these practice sessions, the teachers matched more fluent speakers of English with less fluent speakers to ensure that the newcomer students really understood the purpose and goals of the conferences. During a cross-age session one week, the first-grade students collaborated with their older buddies in writing letters to their parents, inviting them to the interactive conferences; in several pairs, in which the older student could read and write Chinese, the children wrote in both English and Chinese. The teachers also arranged through a local church for Chinese-speaking volunteers to act as translators in the parent-teacher conference component.

At the end of the first day of conferences, the teachers were euphoric. Attendance was almost 100%; the children did a wonderful job of hosting their parents, so that when the parents met with the teachers, they were able to delve into issues in greater depth than ever before; and the volunteer translators found the experience fascinating and exciting. Setting up and preparing for these interactive parent-teacher conferences had been quite time consuming, but everyone agreed that it had been worthwhile. Instead of dreading another day of conferences, as often happens, these first-grade teachers couldn't wait for the next day to dawn.

Conclusion

As you've probably guessed by now, the myths surrounding the education of LEP and language minority students are many and pervasive. Perhaps you've even seen one or two myths represented here that you have heard repeated by those you work with or might have believed yourself.

Unfortunately, these myths can also be quite destructive, as they color the policy, programmatic, and instructional atmospheres in which teachers teach and students learn. We hope that this book will ultimately help dispel some of the myths, make educators more aware of not only the needs, but also the strengths that language minority students bring to the classroom. We further hope that this book will reinforce both the genuinely good intentions and skill that dedicated professionals bring to the education of these kids.

To assist you further in your efforts to uncover the myths and discover the realities, we have included a resource list of agencies and organizations that we have found useful. That list follows.

Resources

National Organizations

The Comprehensive Center Network
Web site: http://www.ncbe.gwu.edu/tan/ccregions.htm
Services: Fifteen Comprehensive Centers are funded by the U.S. Department of Education to provide technical assistance in school reform, coordination of programs for the school success of students, and adoption of promising and proven practices. See the Web site for information regarding individual centers and their respective services.

National Clearinghouse for Bilingual Education (NCBE)
The George Washington University
Center for the Study of Language and Education
2011 Eye Street, NW
Washington, DC 20006
Tel: (202) 467-0867
Fax: (202) 467-4283
Email: askncbe@ncbe.gwu.edu
Web site: http://www://ncbe.gwu.edu
Services: The Clearinghouse is funded by the U.S. Department of Education's Office of Bilingual Education and Minority Language Affairs (OBEMLA) to collect, analyze, and disseminate information related to the education of students from linguistically and culturally diverse backgrounds. Provides a range of resources for educators, including searchable data bases, publications (e.g., a newsletter, reports, and program guides), and an electronic discussion group.

Office of Bilingual Education and Minority Language Affairs (OBEMLA)
U.S. Department of Education
Office of Bilingual Education and Minority Language Affairs
600 Independence Avenue, SW
Washington, DC 20202-6510
Email: obemla@ed.gov
Web site: http://www.ed.gov/offices/OBEMLA
Services: The office is funded to help school districts meet their responsibility to provide an equal educational opportunity to limited English-proficient students. The agency administers programs authorized by Title VII of the Improving American

Schools Act. OBEMLA funds (1) direct instructional services for local educational agencies, (2) support activities that assist schools and school districts in carrying out direct services to students, and (3) professional development programs to increase the supply of teachers and educational personnel trained to work with LEP students. OBEMLA also provides formula-funded grants to state education agencies through the Emergency Immigrant Education Act.

Office of Civil Rights (OCR)
U.S. Department of Education
Office of Civil Rights
Mary Switzer Building
330 C Street, SW
Washington, DC 20202
Tel: (202) 205-5413; (800) 421-3481
Fax: (202) 205-9862
TDD: (202) 205-5166
Email: OCR@ED.gov
Web site: http://www.ed.gov/offices/ocr
Services: OCR is funded by the U.S. Department of Education to ensure equal access to education and to promote educational excellence through vigorous enforcement of civil rights. OCR provides assistance, guidance, and information to students, parents, teachers, and institutions. It also produces publications on civil rights topics.

Center for Applied Linguistics (CAL)
4646 40th Street, NW
Washington, DC 20016-1859
Tel: (202) 362-0700
Fax: (202) 362-3740
Email: info@cal.org
Web site: http://www.cal.org
Services: Works to identify and develop effective educational practices for linguistic and cultural minority students.

Desegregation Assistance Centers
Web site: http://www.umich.edu/~eqtynet
Services: The U.S. Department of Education sponsors ten Desegregation Assistance Centers (DACs) across the country, which help public schools treat all students equally regardless of race, gender or national origin. For information on individual centers, contact the Web site.

National Research and Development Centers

Center on English Learning and Achievement (CELA)
State University of New York
University at Albany
School of Education
1400 Washington Avenue

Albany, NY 12222
Tel: (518) 442-5026
Fax: (518) 442-5933
Web site: http://cela.albany.edu
Services: CELA is one of five national research and development centers funded by the U.S. Department of Education's Office of Educational Research and Improvement. It focuses on the learning and teaching of English (native and nonnative English speakers). It offers publications (e.g., research reports, position papers) and Internet-mediated chat rooms.

Center for Research on Education, Diversity, and Excellence (CREDE)
University of California, Santa Cruz
College Eight, Room 201
1156 High Street
Santa Cruz, CA 95064
Tel: (408) 459-3500
Email: crede@cats.ucsc.edu
Web site: http://www.crede.ucsc.edu
Services: CREDE is one of five national research and development centers funded by the U.S. Department of Education's Office of Educational Research and Improvement. In collaboration with the Center for Applied Linguistics (CAL), the center supports the education of students from diverse backgrounds through conducting research, identifying and developing effective educational practices, and disseminating information through print and other media (e.g., newsletters, research reports, videotapes).

Center for Research on the Education of Students Placed At-Risk (CRESPAR)
Johns Hopkins University, CSOS
3505 North Charles Street
Baltimore, MD 21218
Tel: (410) 516-8800
and
Howard University
Department of Psychology
Washington, DC 20059
Tel: (202) 806-8484
Web site: http://scov.csos.jhu.edu
Services: CRESPAR is one of five national research and development centers funded by the U.S. Department of Education's Office of Educational Research and Improvement. It focuses on students considered at risk of school failure. It disseminates information through a newsletter and reports.

The National Institute for the Education of At-Risk Students (At-Risk Institute)
U.S. Department of Education
OERI/At-Risk Room 610
555 New Jersey Avenue, NW
Washington, DC 20208-5521

Fax: (202) 219-2030
Web site: http://www.ed.gov/offices/OERI/At-Risk
Services: One of five institutes created by the Educational Research, Development, Dissemination and Improvement Act of 1994, and located in the Office of Educational Research and Improvement at the U.S. Department of Education. It sponsors research projects and development activities designed to improve the education of students at risk of educational failure.

Professional Organizations

National Association for Asian and Pacific American Education (NAAPAE)
c/o ARC Associates
1212 Broadway, 4th Floor
Oakland, CA 94612
Tel: (510) 834-9455
Services: This professional organization addresses the educational concerns and needs of Asian and Pacific American students. It publishes a newsletter and anthologies, and sponsors a conference.

National Association for Bilingual Education (NABE)
1220 L Street, NW
Suite 605
Washington, DC 20005-4018
Tel: (202) 898-1829
Web site: http://www.nabe.org
Services: NABE is a professional organization for bilingual educators. It publishes a journal and newsletter, and sponsors an annual convention. It can provide information about state and regional bilingual organizations.

National Association for Multicultural Education (NAME)
1703 Longview Drive
Baton Rouge, LA 70806.
Services: NAME is a professional organization for educators who are interested in promoting multicultural education. NAME has a clearinghouse.

Teachers of English to Speakers of Other Languages (TESOL)
1600 Cameron Street
Suite 300
Alexandria, VA 22314
Tel: (703) 836-0774
Fax: (703) 836-7864
Email: TESOL@tesol.edu
Web site: http://www.tesol.edu
Services: TESOL is a professional organization devoted to the teaching of English to nonnative speakers. It publishes journals, a newspaper and books for teachers, puts on an annual conference, offers staff development throughout the year, and provides placement and career services. TESOL can provide information about state or regional TESOL organizations.

TESLK-12 Listserv
TESLK-12 is intended to facilitate discussion and electronic sharing among teachers of English to children. To join TESLK-12, send a message to LISTSERV@CUNYVM.CUNY.EDU sub TESLK-12 first-name last-name.

Not-for-Profit Advocacy Organizations

Center on Families, Communities, Schools and Children's Learning
3503 N. Charles Street
Baltimore, MD 21218
Tel: (410) 516-0370
Services: The goal of the center is to understand and build partnerships between families, communities, and school, including immigrant communities.

FairTest
342 Broadway
Cambridge, MA 02139
Tel: (617) 964-4810
Fax: (617) 497-2224
Web site: http://www.fairtest.org
Services: The National Center for Fair and Open Testing (FairTest) is an advocacy organization working to end the abuses, misuses, and flaws of standardized testing and ensure that evaluation of students is fair, open, and educationally sound. FairTest provides technical assistance and publishes a newsletter and fact sheets.

National Coalition of Advocates for Students (NCAS)
100 Boylston Street
Suite 737
Boston, MA 02116
Tel: (617) 357-8507
Web site: http://www.ncas1.org
Services: NCAS is a national advocacy organization working on behalf of students in the public schools who are considered vulnerable, including immigrants. Services to the public include the Clearinghouse for Immigrant Education (CHIME), which provides data base searches, bibliographies, informational pamphlets, and other resources devoted to the effective education of immigrant students.

National MultiCultural Institute (NMCI)
3000 Connecticut Avenue, NW
Suite 438
Washington, DC 20009
Web site: http://www.nmci.org
Services: The mission of NMCI is to increase communication, understanding, and respect among people from different backgrounds, and to provide a forum for discussion on related issues. NMCI sponsors conferences and diversity training, and offers resource materials (e.g., books, training manuals).

Local and State Educational Organizations

Colleges or Schools of Education at Local Colleges and Universities
An increasing number of universities and colleges have programs and/or faculty that specialize in the education of language minority students. A call to the college or school can often put you in touch with very knowledgeable resource people.

County and State Offices of Education
Many county and state offices of education provide assistance to districts with language minority students, particularly in areas where large numbers of students acquiring English attend school. Many hire ESOL and bilingual specialists, offer staff development services, and have resource materials that are available for use by area educators.

Glossary

Bilingual—Refers to people who are able to speak two languages with equal skill. Is sometimes used mistakenly to refer to nonfluent speakers of English who are acquiring English as a nonnative language.

Bilingual education—Refers to programs that provide instruction in two languages (e.g., English and Spanish or Chinese).

BINL *(Basic Inventory of Natural Language)*—A language test often used in initial assessment and placement. See Figure 6–4 for a brief description of the test.

BSM *(Bilingual Syntax Measure)*—A language test often used in initial assessment and placement. See Figure 6–4 for a brief description of the test.

Dual language instruction—Nonnative speakers of English and nonnative speakers of another language (usually English speakers) are placed in the same class, and content-area and language instruction is provided in both languages.

ELD *(English language development)*—Refers to classes that are designed for English language learners and usually involves the integration of content-area material with language development.

ELL *(English language learners)*—Refers to nonnative English speakers who are learning English. Many educators prefer this term to other terms (e.g., limited English proficient) because it focuses on what students can do.

ESL *(English as a second language)*—Usually used to refer to a subject area (e.g., "This is an ESL class."), but is sometimes used to refer to students themselves (e.g., ' They are ESL students."). All instruction is in English.

ESOL *(English to speakers of other languages)*—A term that is often used in place of ESL. All instruction is in English.

FEP *(Fluent English proficient)*—Refers to students who may speak a language other than English, but are also fluent in English.

Foreigner talk—Refers to the kind of modified speech that many native speakers of a language use when conversing with a nonnative speaker. May involve simplifying grammatical structures and vocabulary, and speaking more slowly and louder.

IDEA—A language test often used in initial assessment and placement. See Figure 6–4 for a brief description of the test.

L1—First or native language.

L2—Second language; often used in the context of "L2 students," meaning students who are nonnative speakers of a language.

Language minority students—A term that is used by the federal government and other agencies to refer to students who live in homes where a language other than English is spoken. Language minority students may be bilingual, may be acquiring English as a nonnative language, or may be monolingual speakers of English.

LAS *(Language Assessment Scales)*—A language test often used in initial assessment and placement. See Figure 6–4 for a brief description of the test.

LEP *(Limited English proficient)*—A term that is most often used in legal and governmental situations when referring to students learning English as a nonnative language. It includes those students who have learned some English, but are not yet fluent.

NEP *(Non-English proficient)*—Refers to newcomers to English who are just beginning to learn the language.

SDAIE *(Specially designed academic instruction in English)*—Refers to content-area classes taught in English (e.g., science and mathematics) that are designed specifically for ESOL students. The courses are academically rigorous and incorporate techniques that make language and content more accessible to learners (e.g., relying heavily on visuals and role play).

Sheltered English—Specially designed instruction in English for ESOL students that integrates content-area material with language instruction.

Structured immersion—Refers to programs for ESOL students in which only the target language, English, is used for instruction.

TESOL *(Teaching English to Speakers of Other Languages)*—Refers to the discipline of teaching English to nonnative English speakers, including English as a foreign language (EFL). The term is also used to refer to ESOL teachers and a major international professional organization, Teachers of English to Speakers of Other Languages.

Title I—Federal funding designated to support the education of low-achieving, low-income students, including nonnative English-speaking students.

Title VII—Federal funding designated to support the education of low-income, nonnative English-speaking students. In the past, Title VII supported programs that implemented only bilingual instructional models, but in more recent years, funding guidelines have allowed for English-medium instructional models. Also supports programs that provide teacher preparation.

Two-way bilingual education/immersion—Refers to programs in which native and nonnative speakers of English work together, with all students learning content and language through two languages.

References

Ammon, P. 1985. "Helping Children Learn to Write in English as a Second Language: Some Observations and Some Hypotheses." In *The Acquisition of Language: Response and Revision,* ed. S.W. Freedman, 65–84. Norwood, NJ: Ablex.

Arlington Public Schools. April 7, 1993. *News Release: Language Minority Students Achieve Success in New Math Program.* Arlington, VA: Arlington Public Schools.

ASCD Panel on Bilingual Education. 1997. *Building an Indivisible Nation.* Alexandria, VA: Association for Supervision and Curriculum Development.

August, D., K. Hakuta, F. Olguin & D. Pompa. 1995. *LEP Students and Title I: A Guidebook for Educators.* Washington, DC: National Clearinghouse for Bilingual Education.

Baker, K. 1993. "Comments on Suzanne Irujo's Review and Keith Baker's Commentary on *Forked Tongue: The Politics of Bilingual Education.*" *TESOL Quarterly* 27(1): 150–57.

Baker, K. & A. de Kanter. 1981. *Effectiveness of Bilingual Education: A Review of the Literature.* Washington, DC: Office of Planning, Budget and Evaluation, U.S. Department of Education.

———. 1983. *Bilingual Education: A Reappraisal of Federal Policy.* Lexington, MA: Lexington Books.

Barrs, M., S. Ellis, H. Hester & A. Thomas. 1989. *The Primary Language Record.* Portsmouth, NH: Heinemann.

Basic Inventory of Natural Language (BINL). 1979. San Bernardino, CA: CHECpoint Systems.

Baskwill, J. & P. Whitman. 1988. *Evaluation: Whole Language, Whole Child.* NY: Scholastic.

Bialystok, E., ed. 1991. *Language Processing in Bilingual Children.* New York: Cambridge University Press.

Bilingual Syntax Measure (BSM). 1975, 1978. San Antonio, TX: The Psychological Corporation.

Boswell, T.D. 1998. "Implications of Demographic Changes in Florida's Public School Population." In *Creating Florida's Multilingual Global Work Force: Educational Policies and Practices for Students Learning English as a New Language,* ed. S.H. Fradd & O. Lee. Tallahassee: Florida Department of Education.

Brophy, J.E. & T.L. Good. 1974. *Teacher-Student Relationships: Causes and Consequences.* New York: Holt, Rinehart and Winston.

Brown, R. 1973. *A First Language: The Early Stages.* Cambridge, MA: Harvard University Press.

California Department of Education v. San Francisco Unified School District Governing Board, 1998, Superior Court of the State of California in and for the City and County of San Francisco, #994049.

Cantoni-Harvey, G. 1987. *Content-Area Language Instruction.* Reading, MA: Addison-Wesley.

Carew, J.V. & S.L. Lightfoot. 1979. *Beyond Bias: Perspectives on Classrooms.* Cambridge, MA: Harvard University Press.

Carrera, J.W. 1989. *Immigrant Students: Their Legal Right of Access to Public Schools.* Boston, MA: National Coalition of Advocates for Students.

Castañeda v. Pickard, 648 F. 2d 989 (5th Cir. 1981).

Chamot, A.U. & J.M. O'Malley. 1985. *A Cognitive Academic Language Learning Approach.* Rosslyn, VA: National Clearinghouse for Bilingual Education.

———. 1987. "The Cognitive Academic Language Learning Approach: A Bridge to the Mainstream." *TESOL Quarteriy* 21(2): 227–49.

Chamot, A.U., M. Dale, J.M. O'Malley & G.A. Spano. 1992. "Learning and Problem Solving Strategies of ESOL Students." *Bilingual Research Journal* 16(3,4): 1–34.

Chavkin, N.F. 1989. "Debunking the Myth About Minority Parents." *Educational Horizons* (Summer): 119–23.

Chomsky, C. 1969. *The Acquisition of Syntax in Children from 5 to 10.* Cambridge, MA: MIT Press.

Clay, M.M. 1993. *An Observation Survey of Early Literacy Achievement.* Portsmouth, NH: Heinemann.

Coelho, E. 1994. "Social Integration of Immigrant and Refugee Children." In *Language, Culture and Schooling,* ed. F. Genesee, 301–27. New York: Cambridge University Press.

Collier, V.P. 1987. "Age and Rate of Acquisition of Second Language for Academic Purposes." *TESOL Quarterly* 21(4): 617–41.

———. 1989. "How Long? A Synthesis of Research on Academic Achievement in a Second Language." *TESOL Quarterly* 23(3): 509–31.

———. 1992. "A Synthesis of Studies Examining Long-Term Language Minority Student Data on Academic Achievement." *Bilingual Research Journal* 16(1–2): 187–212.

Congressional Quarterly Researcher. August 13, 1993. *Bilingual Education.* Washington, DC: Congressional Quarterly, Inc.

Cook, B. & C. Urzúa. 1993. *The Literacy Club: A Cross-Age Tutoring/Paired Reading Project.* Washington, DC: National Clearinghouse for Bilingual Education.

Crandall, J., ed. 1987. *ESL Through Content Area Instruction: Mathematics, Science, Social Studies.* Englewood Cliffs, NJ: Prentice Hall.

Crawford, J. 1989. *Bilingual Education: History, Politics, Theory and Practice.* Trenton, NJ: Crane Publishing.

Cummins, J. 1979. "Linguistic Interdependence and the Educational Development of Bilingual Children." *Review of Educational Research* 49(2): 222–51.

———. 1981a. "Four Misconceptions About Language Proficiency in Bilingual Education." *NABE Journal* 5(3): 31–45.

———. 1981b. "The Role of Primary Language Development in Promoting Educational Success for Language Minority Students." In *Schooling and Language Minority Students: A Theoretical Framework.* Los Angeles: Evaluation, Dissemination and Assessment Center.

———. 1989. *Empowering Minority Students.* Sacramento: California Association for Bilingual Education.

———. 1991. "Institutionalized Racism and the Assessment of Minority Children: A Comparison of Policies and Programs in the United States and Canada." In *Assessment and Placement of Minority Students,* ed. R.J. Samuda, S.H. Kong, J. Cummins. J. Pascual-Leone & J. Lewis, 95–107. Toronto: C.J. Hogrefe.

Cummins, J. & M. Swain. 1986. *Bilingualism in Education.* New York: Longman.

Cziko, G.A. 1992. "The Evaluation of Bilingual Education: From Necessity and Probability to Possibility." *Educational Researcher* 21(2): 10–15.

Dale, T.C. & G. Cuevas. 1987. "Integrating Language and Mathematics Learning." In *ESL Through Content-Area Instruction: Mathematics, Science, Social Studies,* ed. J. Crandall, 9–54. Englewood Cliffs, NJ: Prentice Hall.

DeVos, G.A. & C. Lee. 1981. *Koreans in Japan.* Berkeley: University of California Press.

Diana v. California State Board of Education, C-7037, Rfp, (U.S. District Court of Northern California, 1970.)

Dulay, H. & M. Burt. 1977. "Natural Sequences in Child Second-Language Acquisition." *Language Learning* 25(1): 37–53.

Dulay, H.C., M.K. Burt & S.D. Krashen. 1982. *Language Two.* New York: Oxford.

Farr, R. & B. Tone. 1998. *Portfolio and Performance Assessment: Helping Students Evaluate Their Progress as Readers and Writers.* 2nd ed. Orlando, FL: Harcourt Brace.

First, J.M. & J.W. Carrerra. 1988. *New Voices: Immigrant Students in the U.S. Public Schools.* Boston, MA: National Coalition of Advocates for Students.

Fleischman, H.L. & P.J. Hopstock. 1993. *Descriptive Study of Services to Limited English Proficient Students.* Development Associates, Inc.: Arlington, VA.

Fountas, I.C. & G.S. Pinnell. 1996. *Guided Reading: Good First Teaching for All Children.* Portsmouth, NH: Heinemann.

Fradd, S.H. & D.K. Wilen. 1990. *Using Interpreters and Translators to Meet the Needs of Handicapped Language Minority Students and Their Families. Program Information Guide 4.* Washington, DC: National Clearinghouse for Bilingual Education.

Friedlander, M. 1991. *The Newcomer Program: Helping Immigrant Students Succeed in U.S. Schools. Program Information Guide 8.* Washington, DC: National Clearinghouse for Bilingual Education.

Gándara, P. & J. Fish. 1994. "Year Round Schooling as an Avenue to Major Structural Reform." *Educational Evaluation and Policy Analysis* 16(1): 67–86.

Gándara, P. & B. Merino. 1993. "Measuring Outcomes of LEP Programs: Test Scores, Exit Rates and Other Mythological Data." *Educational Evaluation and Policy Analysis*, 15(3): 320–38.

General Accounting Office (GAO). 1987. *Bilingual Education: A New Look at the Research Evidence.* Washington, DC: General Accounting Office.

Goodman, Y.M. 1985. "Kidwatching: Observing Children in the Classroom." In *Observing the Language Learner,* ed. A. Jaggar & M.T. Smith-Burke, 9–18. Newark, DE: International Reading Association.

Goodman, Y.M. & A.M. Marek. 1996. *Retrospective Miscue Analysis: Revaluing Readers and Reading.* Katonah, NY: Richard C. Owen.

Goodman, Y.M., D.J. Watson & C.L. Burke. 1987. *Reading Miscue Inventory: Alternative Procedures.* Katonah, NY: Richard C. Owen.

Graves, D.H. & B.S. Sunstein, ed. 1992. *Portfolio Portraits.* Portsmouth, NH: Heinemann.

Guthrie, G.P. 1985. *A School Divided: An Ethnography of Bilingual Education in a Chinese Community.* Hillsdale, NJ: Lawrence Erlbaum.

Hakuta, K. 1986. *Mirror of Language.* New York: Basic Books.

Hakuta, K. & D. August. 1993. *Federal Programs Serving LEP Children: A Blueprint for the Next Generation.* Palo Alto, CA: Stanford Working Group.

Hakuta, K. & L. Gould. 1987. "Synthesis of Research on Bilingual Education." *Educational Leadership* 44(8): 38–45.

Handscombe, J. 1994. "Putting It All Together." In *Educating Second Language Children,* ed. F. Genesee, 331–55. New York: Cambridge University Press.

Heath, S.B. 1983. *Ways with Words.* Cambridge: Cambridge University Press.

———. 1986. "Sociocultural Contexts of Language Development." In *Beyond Language: Social and Cultural Factors in Schooling Language Minority Students,* dev. California State Department of Education, 143–86. Los Angeles: Evaluation, Dissemination and Assessment Center, California State University, Los Angeles.

Hoffman, D.M. & S.B. Heath. 1986. *Inside Learners: Guidebook on Interactive Reading and Writing in Elementary Classrooms.* Palo Alto, CA: Stanford University.

Hudelson, S. 1994. "Literacy Development of Second Language Children." In *Educating Second Language Children,* ed. F. Genesee, 129–58. New York: Cambridge University Press.

Hudelson, S. & I. Serna. April, 1993. "Literacy and Language Choice in Bilingual/Second Language Classrooms." Paper presented at the Annual Meeting of Teachers of English to Speakers of Other Languages, Atlanta, GA.

IDEA Oral Language Proficiency Test (IPT). 1978, 1994. Brea, CA: Ballard & Tighe.

Jacobson, L. August 5, 1998. "Hispanic Children Outnumber Young Blacks for 1ˢᵗ Time." *Education Week on the Web.* <http://www.edweek.org>

Kagan, S. 1986. "Cooperative Learning and Sociocultural Factors in Schooling." In *Beyond Language: Social and Cultural Factors in Schooling Language Minority Students,* dev. California State Department of Education, 231–98. Los Angeles: Evaluation, Dissemination and Assessment Center, California State University, Los Angeles.

Kemp, M. 1987. *Watching Children Read and Write: Observational Records for Children with Special Needs.* Portsmouth, NH: Heinemann.

Kessler, C. & M.E. Quinn. 1987. "ESL and Science Learning." In *ESL Through Content-Area Instruction: Mathematics, Science, Social Studies,* ed. J. Crandall, 55–88. Englewood Cliffs, NJ: Prentice Hall.

Keyes v. School District No. 1 of Denver, Colorado, 576 F. Supp. 1503, 1510 D. Col. 1983.

King, M., B. Fagan, T. Bratt & R. Baer. 1987. "ESL and Social Studies Instruction." In *ESL Through Content-Area Instruction: Mathematics, Science, Social Studies,* ed. J. Crandall, 89–121. Englewood Cliffs, NJ: Prentice Hall.

Krashen, S. 1981. *Second Language Acquisition and Second Language Learning.* Oxford: Pergamon.

———. July, 1998. "Bilingual Education and the Dropout Argument." *Discover,* 4. Washington, DC: National Clearinghouse for Bilingual Education.

Language Assessment Scales (LAS). 1978, 1991. Monterey, CA: CTB Macmillan McGraw-Hill.

Lau v. Nichols, 414 U.S. 563, 94 S. Ct. 786, 39 L. Ed. 2d1 1974.

Lindfors, J.W. 1989. "The Classroom: A Good Environment for Language Learning." In *When They Don't All Speak English,* ed. P. Rigg & V.G. Allen. Urbana, IL: National Council of Teachers of English.

Lindholm, K. 1987. *Directory of Bilingual Immersion Programs: Two Way Bilingual Education for Language Minority and Majority Students.* Los Angeles: Center for Language Education and Research.

Long, M.H. & A. Porter. 1985. "Group Work, Interlanguage Talk, and Second Language Acquisition." *TESOL Quarterly* 19(2): 207–27.

Lucas, T., R. Henze & R. Donato. 1990. "Promoting the Success of Latino Language Minority Students: An Exploratory Study of Six High Schools." *Harvard Educational Review,* 60(3): 315–40.

Macías, R. 1989. *The National Need for Bilingual Teachers.* Claremont, CA: Tomás Rivera Policy Institute.

Matute-Bianchi, M.E. 1986. "Ethnic Identities and Patterns of School Success Among Mexican-Descent and Japanese-American Students in a California High School: An Ethnographic Analysis." *American Journal of Education* 95: 233–55.

McKeon, D. 1994. "Language, Culture and Schooling." In *Language, Culture and Schooling,* ed. F. Genesee, 15–32. New York: Cambridge University Press.

McKeon, D. & L. Malarz. 1991. *School Based Management: What Bilingual and ESL*

Program Directors Should Know. Washington, DC: National Clearinghouse for Bilingual Education.

Menacker, J., E. Hurwitz & W. Weldon. 1988. "Parent-Teacher Cooperation in Schools Serving the Urban Poor." *The Clearing House* 62(3): 108–12.

Meyer, M. & S. Feinberg, ed. 1992. *Assessing Evaluation Studies: The Case of Bilingual Education Strategies.* Washington, DC: National Research Council.

Minicucci, C. & L. Olsen. 1992. *Programs for Secondary LEP Students: A California Study.* Washington, DC: National Clearinghouse for Bilingual Education.

Mohan, B.A. 1986. *Language and Content.* Reading, MA: Addison-Wesley.

Moll, L. 1992. "Literacy Research in Community and Classrooms: A Sociocultural Approach." In *Multidisciplinary Perspectives on Literacy Research,* ed. R. Beach, J.L. Green, M.L. Kamil & T. Shanahan. Urbana, IL: National Council of Teachers of English.

National Board for Professional Teaching Standards. 1996. *English as a New Language: Draft Standards for National Board Certification.* Washington, DC: National Board for Professional Teaching Standards.

National Commission on Teaching and America's Future. 1996. *What Matters Most: Teaching for America's Future.* New York: Teachers College, Columbia University.

National Council of Teachers of English & International Reading Association. 1996. *Standards for the English Language Arts.* Urbana, IL: National Council of Teachers of English & Newark, DL: International Reading Association.

Navarrete, C., J. Wilde, C. Nelson, R. Martinez & G. Hargett. 1990. *Informal Assessment in Educational Evaluation: Implications for Bilingual Education Programs.* Washington, DC: National Clearinghouse for Bilingual Education.

Ogbu, J.U. 1992. "Understanding Cultural Diversity and Learning." *Educational Researcher* 21(8): 5–14.

Ogbu, J.U. & M.E. Matute-Bianchi. 1986. "Understanding Socio-Cultural Factors: Knowledge, Identity and School Adjustment." In *Beyond Language: Social and Cultural Factors in Schooling Language Minority Students,* dev. California State Department of Education, 73-142. Los Angeles: Evaluation, Dissemination and Assessment Center, California State University, Los Angeles.

O'Malley, J.M. & D. Waggoner. 1984. "Public School Teacher Preparation and the Teaching of ESL." *TESOL Newsletter* 18(3): 1, 18–22.

Ovando, C. & V.P. Collier. 1985. *Bilingual and ESL Classrooms: Teaching in Multicultural Contexts.* New York: McGraw-Hill.

Oxford, R.L. 1992/1993. "Language Learning Strategies in a Nutshell: Update and ESL Suggestions." *TESOL Journal* 2(2): 18–22.

Pease-Álvarez, L., E. García & P. Espinosa. 1991. "Effective Instruction for Language Minority Students: An Early Childhood Case Study." *Early Childhood Research Quarterly* 6: 347–61.

Peña v. Board of Education of City of Atlanta, 620 F. Supp. 293 1985.

Penfield, J. 1987. "ESL: The Regular Teachers' Perspective. *TESOL Quarterly* 21(1): 21–39.

Pierce, L.V. & M. O'Malley. 1992. *Performance Assessment and Portfolio Assessment for Language Minority Students.* Washington, DC: National Clearinghouse for Bilingual Education.

Plyler v. Doe, 457 U.S. 202 1982.

Prince, C.D. & J.A. Hubert. 1994. "Measuring the Cost of Bilingual Education." *The Journal of Educational Issues of Language Minority Students* 13: 121–35.

Ramirez, J. 1992. "Executive Summary." *Bilingual Research Journal* 16(1–2): 1–62.

Ramirez, J.D., S.D. Yuen, D.R. Ramey. D.J. Pasta & D.K. Billings. 1991. *Longitudinal Study of Structured English Immersion Strategy, Early-Exit and Late-Exit Transitional Bilingual Education Programs for Language Minority Children.* Washington, DC: U.S. Office of Policy and Planning.

Rhodes, L.K., ed. 1993. *Literacy Assessment: A Handbook of Instruments.* Portsmouth, NH: Heinemann.

Rist, R.C. 1970. "Student Social Class and Teacher Expectations: The Self-Fulfilling Prophecy in Ghetto Education." *Harvard Educational Review* 40(3): 411–51.

Rivera, C. & A. Vehler. 1990. *Assuring the Academic Success of Language Minority Students: Collaboration in Teaching and Learning.* Arlington, VA: Development Associates.

Rosenthal, R. & L. Jacobson. 1968. *Pygmalion in the Classroom.* New York: Holt, Rinehart and Winston.

Samuda, R.J. 1991. "Towards Nondiscriminatory Assessment: Principles and Application." In *Assessment and Placement of Minority Students,* ed. R.J. Samuda, S.H. Kong, J. Cummins, J. Pascual-Leone & J. Lewis, 95–107. Toronto: C. J. Hogrefe.

Samway, K. Davies. 1993a. "'This Is Hard, Isn't It?': Children Evaluating Writing." *TESOL Quarterly* 27(2): 233–58.

———. 1993b. *Writers' Workshop and Children Acquiring English as a Non-Native Language.* Washington, DC: National Clearinghouse for Bilingual Education.

———. 1994. "But It's Hard to Keep Fieldnotes While Also Teaching." *TESOL Journal* 4(1): 47–48.

Samway, K. Davies, G. Whang, & M. Pippitt. 1995. *Buddy Reading: Cross-Age Tutoring in a Multicultural, Multilingual School.* Portsmouth, NH: Heinemann.

Saville-Troike, M. 1991. *Teaching and Testing for Academic Achievement: The Role of Language Development.* (Occasional Paper in Bilingual Education.) FOCUS No. 4. Washington, DC: National Clearinghouse for Bilingual Education.

Scarcella, R. 1989. *Teaching Language Minority Students in the Multicultural Classroom.* Englewoods Cliffs, NJ: Prentice Hall Regents.

Schinke-Llano, L. 1983. "Foreigner Talk in Content Classrooms." In *Classroom Centered Research in Second Language Acquisition,* ed. H. Selinger & M.H. Long, 146–65. Rowley, MA: Newbury House.

Schweers, C.W. & J.A. Vélez. 1992. "To Be or Not to Be Bilingual in Puerto Rico: That Is the Issue." *TESOL Journal* 2(1): 13–16.

Simich-Dudgeon, C., ed. 1986. *Issues of Parent Involvement.* Proceedings of symposium held at Trinity College, Washington, DC.

Slavin, R.E. 1990. *Cooperative Learning: Theory, Research, and Practice.* NJ: Prentice Hall.

Snow, M.A., M. Met, & F. Genessee. 1989. "A Conceptual Framework for the Integration of Language and Content in Second/Foreign Language Instruction." *TESOL Quarterly* 23(2): 201–17.

Staffing the Multilingually Impacted Schools of the 1990's: National Forum on Personnel Needs for Districts with Changing Demographics. 1990. Washington, DC: Office of Bilingual Education and Minority Language Affairs OBEMLA, U.S. Department of Education.

Stewart, D.W. 1993. *Immigration and Education: The Crisis and Opportunities.* New York: Lexington Books.

Syvanen, C. 1993. "Team Teaching in Second Grade: Don't Pull out the Kids, Push in the Teacher." In *Common Threads of Practice: Teaching English to Children Around the World,* ed. K. Davies Samway & D. McKeon. Alexandria, VA: Teachers of English to Speakers of Other Languages.

Taylor, D.M. 1990. "Writing and Reading Literature in a Second Language." In *Workshop 2: Beyond the Basal,* ed. N. Atwell, 105–17. Portsmouth, NH: Heinemann.

Teachers of English to Speakers of Other Languages. 1997. *ESL Standards for Pre-K–12 students.* Alexandria, VA: Teachers of English to Speakers of Other Languages.

———. 1998. *Managing the Assessment Process: A Framework for Measuring Student Attainment of the ESL Standards.* Alexandria, VA: Teachers of English to Speakers of Other Languages.

Teresa P. v. Berkeley Unified School District. (California, 1989).

Tierney, R.J., M.A. Carter & L.E. Desai. 1991. *Portfolio Assessment in the Reading-Writing Classroom.* Norwood, NJ: Christopher-Gordon.

Tikunoff, W.J., B.S. Ward, D. van Broekhuizen, et al. 1991. *A Descriptive Study of Significant Features of Exemplary Special Alternative Instructional Programs Executive Summary.* Los Alamitos, CA: Southwest Regional Educational Laboratory.

Trueba, H.T. 1984. "The Forms, Functions and Values of Literacy: Reading for Survival in a Barrio as a Student." *NABE Journal* 9: 21–38.

Urzúa, C. 1987. "'You Stopped Too Soon': Second Language Children Composing and Revising." *TESOL Quarterly* 21(2): 297–304.

Valencia, S.W. 1998. *Literacy Portfolios in Action.* Orlando, FL: Harcourt Brace.

Violand-Sánchez, E., C.P. Sutton & H.W. Ware. 1991. *Fostering Home-School Cooperation: Involving Language Minority Families as Partners in Education.* Washington, DC: National Clearinghouse for Bilingual Education.

Wells, G. 1986. *The Meaning Makers: Children Learning Language and Using Language to Learn.* Portsmouth, NH: Heinemann.

Willig, A.C. 1985. "A Meta-analysis of Selected Studies on the Effectiveness of Bilingual Education." *Review of Educational Research* 55(3): 269–317.

Wong Fillmore, L. 1976. *The Second Time Around: Cognitive and Social Strategies in Second Language Acquisition.* Unpublished dissertation, Stanford University.

Woodward, H. 1994. *Negotiated Evaluation: Involving Children and Parents in the Process.* Portsmouth, NH: Heinemann.

Index